Stumbling Blocks Become Stepping Stones With Jesus

Finé Pienaar

Writers Club Press
San Jose New York Lincoln Shanghai

Stumbling Blocks Become Stepping Stones With Jesus

Writers Club Press
an imprint of iUniverse, Inc.

For information address:
iUniverse, Inc.
5220 S. 16th St., Suite 200
Lincoln, NE 68512
www.iuniverse.com

ISBN: 0-595-25013-0

Printed in the United States of America

Contents

Foreword and acknowledgements

All Bible quotations are from the New International Version (NIV) or the Amplified Bible.

God's favor: for now !!

The miraculous testimonies I am recounting in the latter part of this book, is a great tribute to my Heavenly Father, Jesus Christ the Son of God, and the Precious Holy Spirit! MY praise and thanksgiving is boundless! I am totally dependent upon Jesus, and I am really glad, that He said in:**John 15.5 "(without) apart from Me you can do nothing."**

My friend, Esther Bowman, asked me a question, that caused me to think, and think deeply. She wanted to know, when the last miracle had happened, before I got to Colorado Springs in April 2002

Confronted by such a question, I began to think back. Truthfully, I can say, that not a single day passes, without miracles. Even when I ask for parking in a very congested place, surely, if I had remembered to ask beforehand, favor, His favor, gives me a parking space! We tend to look at **"Big"** things, according to **Our** insight, and overlook the miracles right before or eyes!

To be able to see the clouds on the mountain, **to be able to walk and run!** To **jump for joy, to hear** the rustle of the wind, and the laugh of a baby, **to smell** the lovely scent of **a rose,** to have **the love of my children, grandchildren and friends!** A nice **bed, a warm bath, enough food! OH! All these are miracles!** Given because of HIS favor. My list of miracles never ends! **Most of all, to be** ever, acutely aware and **sure, that His love, mercy and favor surrounds me All the time!**

My dear son, Karel, beautiful daughter in law, Cherie, and lovely granddaughter, Savannah lives in Minneapolis. I kept confessing, since January, that I would be able to go to them at the end of March, or the beginning of April!

I did not have the means to do that! A spiritual daughter of mine, Elsie prophesied to me. She knew not that I talked to the Lord, about my accounts! She told me, the Lord said, I am not to look at the accounts, and say: "This is Facts, because, **facts is not faith!**"

Therefore, I started believing that the Lord would provide the means to come to the States! My son provided tickets for me, to Minneapolis, and to Colorado Springs and here I am! This is but two of the miracles before I was in Colorado Springs.

At the travel agency, they told me that the ticket would be R2000 cheaper if I stayed 6months.Should I come back before or later,I would have to pay a fine of R600. [Our South African money.] Still R1400 cheaper!.When I heard about the six months option, I smiled, and said: "Lord, I think You are aware of something I do not know. I sense in my Spirit that You, Lord have a share in this!"

From Minneapolis I came to Colorado Springs, because I have already known Bruce and Esther Bowman for 24 years! I could not go back home without seeing them! Now, allow me to tell you about some of the stumbling blocks, I encountered here, and how the Lord, turned them into Stepping Stones!

When I arrived, I shared some of my "stories' with Christians. They were so encouraged, that they told me to write a book, to relate my **"TRUE STORIES." "It so happened,"** that my friend, **Bruce, had a spare computer. He set it up** in my room, for **me to start writing the book**. It happened so quickly, before I could say **NO,** I was typing!

Let me emphatically state, that I enjoy and admire the cleverly devised plots, most writers use in books. To be able to fathom the total story, from the beginning, to the end, intrigues me! That is definitely NOT the case with this book! I "lived and experienced" most of the testimonies! I do not have to conjure up scenes and plots, because ALL of it is true! I only relate what happened! So, you may relax, enjoy, and praise the Lord for His Love, Goodness, and involvement with HIS children!

I started writing with a lot of Gusto. (The dictionary meaning is: keen enjoyment, enthusiasm, or relish!) **Ignorance,** dear reader, is **Not bliss in my case!** A lot of testimonies, that I laboriously typed on the computer, disappeared, because of lack of knowledge! I had to do them all over again!

I came from a very **High stress situation,** because of the crime rate in South Africa. **Every time they fired the canon at** Sky Sox stadium for runs, I **jumped!** If it happens in my country, somebody was fired at, or killed! Therefore, I **first had to relax, and come into His peace, the peace, that passes all understanding.**

Two very special persons, P, and M, have a wonderful ministry. They have a retreat, for weary, wounded and battle-scarred people who are in ministry. Soon after I arrived in Colorado Springs, they invited me to spend a few days in the "HAVEN." It was as beneficial as cool water, to someone dying from thirst in the desert. They spoiled me totally! What their hospitality meant to me is indescribable! They live nearly 6000 feet above the city, on the mountains, near Pikes Peak, surrounded by the beauty of nature!

I appreciated P overmuch, because, he took me all the way to Cripple Creek, and around the fantastic mountains. OH! **I cannot describe how I enjoyed the trip.** He was able to tell me all kinds of detail, that anybody driving through, could not have guessed, and enjoyed, as I did! **May God Bless you abundantly my brother!**

The first two nights there, I could not sleep at all! My bed was next to the window, and I became an avid "Stargazer!" Being so high, without city lights, the stars seemed huge and clear; like prismatic diamonds, sparkling in the firmament! Clearer than I have ever seen!

The quietude, peace, and my awareness of the wondrous beauty of the night and star spangled sky, was so totally overwhelming, that I could not jeopardize it by sleeping. I was rejuvenated! I was restored!

Healed, and invigorated! My whole being, could reach out, drink in, taste, enjoy, and experience the presence and goodness of God! It flowed throughout my being! Liquid Love! Sometimes, I prayed. Sometimes I wept! Sometimes I laughed! Sometimes I was just filled with His wonder! Or just looked, in amazement! Drinking in the beauty of it all! **Could this be real? Really Me, enjoying such special favor?** Praise God!

To be able to open up all recesses within, with NO reserve, before His All seeing eyes, and to be aware of His total knowledge of ME. My ups, my downs, my hopes, my failures, my desires, my longings, my strivings, my trials, my trails, my emptiness, yes, **my dire need of HIM**, who is **My all in all!** Cleansed, washed by tears! Hope! Yes! **Filled with fresh, new Hope!** OH Yes! Yes! **He IS,** and ever will be, **The source,** the **Only source of Hope and Love!**

Who Deserve such love and hospitality? I certainly did not feel that I, in the least qualified! BUT, then, **who could ever qualify?** NO I cannot even use the word in the context of the Love of God, Jesus my redeemer, Or the precious comforter! **We cannot Deserve** anything!

The realization, that **All is just His Mercy, Grace and LOVE!** We cannot, earn ANY of that! To lie back, to watch the stars and **to experience Psalm 103.13 "For as high as the heavens are above the earth, SO GREAT is HIS LOVE for those who fear Him; 12. As far as the east is from the west, so far has He removed our transgressions from us. 13. As a father has compassion on his children, so has the Lord compassion on those who fear Him. 14. For He knows our frame He earnestly remembers and imprints [on His heart] that we are DUST.**

No claim to Fame, **No claim to anything but to His love,** and only **because Jesus paid for it with His Own precious blood!**

To lie back in bed, **No!, to lie back, in the Everlasting arms!** To cease from struggle, cease from self, cease from worry, cease from planning, **only to Be!** To Be lost **In HIM!** To Melt and Merge, as it is, **into His fullness**, His total provision! To float on HIS liquid love!

There is no need in Him! HE Is More Than Enough! OH! How I enjoyed and appreciated the Bountiful, beautiful NIGHTS!

The third night, Father planned some sleep for me, because He knew I needed it! The sky, was totally overcast, **No stars were visible!** I slept deeply, catching up on sleep I "Lost" the two previous nights. I woke up totally refreshed!

I casually looked through the window. **What! A Glorious Surprise!** I was In A **Wonderland of Snow!** OH! The beauty of it! A white veil lay over everything! Clean, clear, virgin snow! **What an experience!** We last had snow in Johannesburg, in 1982! I could but look, and look, and admire! The glorious mountains, were so picturesque in their whiteness, and brilliance. The air was crisp, clear, and Cold! **God, our Heavenly Father, has thousands of ways to surprise us! He likes to spoil us, and He wants us to enjoy all of His creation, and works!** You can be sure, I certainly did, to the utmost of my ability!

On Sunday, we went down the mountains, to church. **All the way, I could but gaze in ecstasy** at the pure, picturesque beauty of the mountains, homes, and trees, clad in snow! Thank You, Lord, for giving me such a treat. Thank you, my friends, that I could enjoy your love and hospitality! It is recorded in heaven and only God, can, and will repay you, for what you did for me! It was indeed: "Stepping Stones" that led to a glorious fellowship with the Lord, and with them! This fellowship will endure for eternity!

When I got to Colorado Springs, my glasses started hurting my nose. I went to a few opticians, and twice did they put on new nose "studs". They adjusted it four times, but it did not stop hurting. I said to Esther, I wonder if the Lord is trying to tell me, that I need new glasses? However, with our poor South African money exchange rate, everything has to be multiplied by ten! $1.00 cost ten of our Rands! So, I tried to get glasses at a reasonable price, but it worked out three times more expensive, than it would cost me, in my country! So I tried to get by!

My friends, with whom I am "staying,' have a very cute, clever little dog. He inspires me to get exercise, because he loves to go for a walk with me. On one walking expedition, the stop of the leash broke! He had a free, wild run, with yards and yards of rope! I tried to gather the rope together, to shorten his running scope, when he suddenly stopped at a tree!

I was concentrating totally on gathering the rope, therefore, when he rushed off with a terrific speed, his sudden rush, caught me off guard, and jerked me forward. **My feet slipped, and in an instant,** like lightning, **I was Down! Flat Down! My Face,** was being **ground onto the sidewalk.** The left glass, of **my glasses got scratched beyond repair!** My face was hurting excruciatingly, and I thought it to be bleeding profusely. I could not touch it, because I had my hands full of rope, trying to hold onto Theo, the little doggy! Two people came to help me up, I surely must have been a sight, for sore eyes, stretched out flat on my face!

The moment I crashed onto the cement, and realized the damage to my glasses, I said: **"Well, Lord,** is this another car episode?" **Does ALL things work together for good?** The fall too? **I believe it will, because Your Word says so,** even though I do not know how! I did not plan the fall nor the scratch!

Peter, my husband was a real "absentminded professor" We had to go out one evening, and, because he was sick and not always concentrating well, I did not want him to drive. However, he insisted on driving! When he stopped, **he Scratched our car!** I promise you, I had a lot, a fat big lot, of negative things I could have said, but decided against it! Instead, I kept my mouth shut, but inwardly I said: **"Lord, for the life of me, I cannot see how?** But, **Your Word says in: Rom. 8.28 "And we know that All THINGS work together for good to them that love God. "**I love YOU, and **I am going to stay in Your Word,** and believe that **it will work for our good.** As You, Lord, alone, know how!" I estimated the cost of repairs at about R1000, or more! A VERY big BLOW!

At the Body shop, [we call it panel beater, in South Africa,] the owner said, that it was a very small problem, it would be only R100.00. One tenth of the R1000! (our tithes to God, is one tenth, He gives us, nine tenths.) This had happened, to enable us to buy a car, at a third of the price it should have been! God brought us to the body shop to get a better, virtually new car! The odometer, showed only 4000 kilometers! It even smelled like a new car! A sticker I saw on another car read "Let us not meet by accident!" God in his favor, had changed the accident, into a very good meeting! Back to the glasses!

My friend, Esther, called Lens Crafters, to find out if they could make me one lens according to the prescription. She told the assistant what my problem was, but it was not possible. The lens and bifocal could not be made that way. He told her to phone Lions Club to ask for help. She sent them a fax telling them the story, about my being a missionary, a widow and about the exchange rate not in my favor. A song in our country says: "I'd rather be seventy years young, than to be forty years **Old!'** Well, I'm not too far from the seventy years young!

The Lions Club, had a meeting, where they related my story, and two very special people, "adopted" me. You will find out, in the rest of the book, that I had been at the giving end, most of our lives, but had to learn to receive because we lost all our money. The Bible says it is more blessed to give, than to receive. It is definitely Not easy, to ask! Thank you so much, Esther, that you asked for me! Bless you, abundantly!

I do not want to embarrass the dear persons who offered to pay for the glasses, by using their names. They were only instrumental to get me to the wonderful, sympathetic optometrist who paid for the tinting [transition lenses,] bifocals, frame and the eye test. I just want to tell everyone, that **I received the best glasses, treatment and eye exam I ever had.** I can see extremely well! I can even see to the top of the mountain, Pikes Peak, and even further, **I definitely see far into the future!** Yes! I see how I will bless them, and pray for God's blessings for them, the dear people, every day, **when I use, enjoy**

and Appreciate this glasses! Thank you again, a million times! **May God Bless you always!**

Stumbling blocks? OH Yes! However, with Jesus it became Stepping Stones to new glasses for me! However, God had in mind much more, when I was lying on the sidewalk, flat on my face, hurt and perplexed! I'm sure He smiled, knowing what He had up His sleeve! He knows the end from the beginning.

I met the sweet lady who adopted me, and a dear friend of hers, and we had wonderful communion with each other. We shared testimonies of our Heavenly Father's love, mercy and provision! Definitely more than glasses are involved here! Somebody told me in Colorado Springs, that **God is a "multi purpose God!"** I cannot agree more! It is like throwing a pebble into a dam. The circles evolve ever wider! I did not orchestrate this Symphony! And it still is unfinished!

I met an extremely precious lady, Wanda, in 1987, the first time we came to Colorado Springs. She has a prayer meeting at her home every Tuesday morning. I asked Esther, my landlady, to take me to the prayer meeting, to renew our friendship and love!.

Words definitely cannot describe the precious presence of the Sweet Holy Spirit in the meetings! With our Christian family, it does not seem as if ten or more years had passed since we saw each other! We just continued where we left off! What a privilege!

The fellowship we enjoyed, the love and joy in the Lord, is indescribable! I could not agree more, when Barbara said that she is a fervent admirer of God's handiwork! So am I! The flowers, the trees, the mountain,all is extremely beautiful. However the greatest beauty of all His creation, is His precious children. WAH! How I enjoyed them!

Thank you for what you sowed into my life! Most of the ladies, are seniors like me, but that does not make us without whit or joy!

We shared testimonies of answered prayer every week! How wonderful it is to realize that we still can agree with Jesus as he said at the grave of Lazarus: I thank You that You always hear Me!Let me just state how much I appreciated, and still do, to have been accepted as part of their fellowship. They promised to "adopt" me, and to pray for the ministry God has called me to. It is so wonderful to have back-up prayer!

May God bless the lady who played the piano so beautifully, thank you Georgia! We also had a feast at their home. I have never seen so much food together for a pick-nick! Their hospitality, was absolutely fantastic! There must have been between two and three hundred people!It certainly was a very enjoyable occasion! Thank You Barbara, for your special blessing!

Thank you Wanda, for all you did and meant to me. God bless you, thank you that God's special love can flow through you so beautifully! **Bless you Abundantly!**

Testimonies from another Christian.

I am enclosing two testimonies from somebody else, just to illustrate, that miracles happen to lots of other believers too. I do not claim to be the only one to enjoy His miracles, love and intervention!

In 1988 Cheryl R was a single mother of four children. She was unable to work, because of two back injuries. They had to trust the Lord for all their needs, and provision.

One Saturday morning, they were without most of what they needed. She and her kids, made out a shopping list, of all that was necessary! They needed nylons and all the other items, girls usually need.

They listed, that toothpaste, and toilet paper was essential! They specified the food they needed, and told the Lord that guma-mints, was not a need, but that they would like to have some.

A friend, of her, Johna drove past a lady who was selling flowers. Sitting nearby, was another lady, with two daughters, holding a sign asking for food! Johna, was filled with sympathy, and quickly went to a store. She bought everything the Lord laid on her heart, a whole trolley-cart full. She then drove to where she had seen the lady, to give her the food!

She looked for the lady, but there was no sign of her. Johna, asked the lady who sold flowers, if she knew who the lady was, or where she had gone to.

The lady selling the flowers, said she hadn't seen any lady or children. Even, when Johna insisted that they had been sitting just a few feet away from her, holding a sign asking for food, she denied it emphatically!

Johna, went home, confused and disappointed, because **she had been so sure God had prompted her to buy the food,** and all other items.

She called another friend, and asked her, what she should do with the things she had purchased. This friend, mentioned Sheryl and her kids. Hesitantly, Johna called Sheryl, because she did not want to offend her. She told her about the food, and why she had bought it, and Sheryl gladly accepted her offer to have the food!

She brought all the stuff to Sheryl. The carry bags were laden, it contained every one of the items that were on the shopping list, they had presented to the Lord. The monthly items the girls had requested, were the expensive brands they preferred, but were unable to buy, because they always chose the least expensive, for lack of money!.

They all rejoiced, when they compared the list, with all Johna had bought, and they praised God, for the miraculous way He had inspired Johna to buy the items. She bought everything on the list, even the guma mints!

That same year, they had another miracle, at Christmas time. Sheryl and her children, had nothing in their cupboards, and nothing in their stomachs as well. She wanted the kids to experience the awesome providing Spirit of God, and the real meaning of Christmas! They were going to spend Christmas at their Grandpa's house, and were feeling bad that they could not contribute anything. They would just open their presents, eat and do the dishes!

Sheryl, spent some time talking to the Lord about the situation. He gave her some Scriptures: **Isiah 30.21 And your ears shall hear a** word behind you, saying, This is the way, walk in it, when you turn to the right hand and when you turn to the left."

When the Lord told her that he would tell her which way to go, she listened! He instructed her, to organize a Christmas party at her house, each of them had to invite two friends. She was not sure that she had heard right, or was her mind playing her tricks? How could they have a party, when they did not even have food for themselves! Well, **everything is possible to him that believe**s. So, she believed enough to listen some more!

The Lord gave her the menu of the dinner she was to cook! He said: "fix ham, baked potatoes, with sour cream, broccoli with cheese sauce, a relish tray, and pretzel dessert (her favorite)" and a few more things.

She argued with the Lord. **BAKED POTATOES!** Baked potatoes need to be perfect, but it would not matter if they were mashed. Pretzel dessert! That costs a lot of money! Relish tray! She argued, but then decided to believe, and start doing what He had told her!

Next, she said she would like to have a Christmas tree! He instructed her to clean the house, and arrange the furniture to make room. They got busy to do what He said!That night, a friend came by, and took her daughter to buy a tree. But what about decorations for the tree? She decided to make some snowflakes with colored popcorn. She bought material for $1.00, and made cloth ornaments.

Before they were back with the tree, somebody else knocked! It was a friend, she brought wonderful lights and decorations. It had never been used, and was going to be thrown away, if Sheryl had no use for it on their tree!. WOW! What a beautiful tree they had!

The day for the party was coming closer, food and money was pretty much gone! How in the world could she give a party for fifteen guests! Same scripture: **Everything is possible for them who believes!** The night before the party, they were really hungry, there was only flour and water. **No one had anything to eat!**

Her daughter yelled: "Where is this God you tell us about? **I want fruit, and I want it NOW!**"

Sheryl told her to go to her room, and ask God where the food is. She said that it did not always have to be only her faith and prayers.

Fifteen minutes later, she came back and said: "I'm sorry Mom, **God said that before the night is over, I will eat all the fruit I want!**" Her two daughters went off to a youth meeting. Sheryl kept reaching for the phone, **thinking to cancel the party. Maybe she did not hear God at all?** What if it was something she had made up in her mind? The enemy, were bringing her all kinds of thoughts. However, **every time she touched the phone, she remembered** God's promises and **Mark 9 23: "All things are possible to him that believe."** SHE CHOSE TO BELIEVE !

Around nine thirty, the girls came home, and placed a very large box on the table, closed with gift wrap. They told her, as they were driving out of the parking lot, **a lady** stopped the car, and **asked if they were Tanya and Tamara?** They said Yes. **The Lady said: "Here is a box for your Mother."**

Excitedly, they opened the box! **Amazing! A Miracle! In it was everything** on the menu **for the party, and food for a week.**

There were, 20 perfectly big round baking potatoes, 20 oranges, 20 bananas, 20 apples, 20 grapefruit and every other kind of fruit imaginable! **AND!** There was the nicest ham, broccoli, cheese, carrots, celery, radishes, pickles, olives, and everything else needed for a relish tray. In the box were also, pretzels, cream cheese, whipping cream, jell o, and strawberries! All the ingredients to make her favorite Pretzel Dessert. OHHH! AHA! God is very GOOD! He keeps his promises!

They still think that the lady with the box, was an angel! It must have been a heavy box, with all the fruit, and food in it. They did not know her, the parking lot was empty, and the church closed, by the time the girls came to their car to go home.

I would say it was a Special delivery, in answer to prayer. Our God is a God who can answer by fire, to devour the Priests of Baal, or by providing food for his hungry kids! Our God is definitely a multipurpose God! Stumbling blocks does not intimidate Him.

I had a desire to visit friends of mine in Albuquerque. They used to stay in South Africa. When they wanted to emigrate to the US, she kept on confessing that they were going to leave before Christmas. They have five children, so they had to have tickets for seven people! They also needed a sponsor, or they could not come! Her faith was a beacon of light, and on Christmas eve, I took them to the airport, to board for the US. Because nobody desires to fly during Christmas, the Lord gave them favor, **they got a big** discount on their tickets. A Church also sponsored them.

Cheryl drove me to see them! I am so abundantly thankful that she did that. May the Lord bless her household abundantly! Thanks also to her husband who formatted the book, and corrected the margins. May God bless you supernaturally for the time you spent doing that.

We spent a lovely time together. They told me about things the Lord did for them, since we last saw each other, and so did I!

While in Colorado Springs, I made a commitment, I told the Lord that I would no longer do secular work in South Africa. The need is so horrendously big. Thousands are dying of Aids per week. To think of them going to hell is exceedingly painful. I am going to preach the Gospel and pray for the healing of the sick. God promised to heal the aids patients, should they repent! Dear reader, please remember me in your prayers.

I want to thank all who took me to lunch, breakfast and dinner. May The Lord bless you richly! Not only for the food, but for your love and fellowship too! Marti, you are an inspiration, you blessed me tremendously with your singing and the way you play the piano a revelation! Thanks for sharing with me, your testimony and the delicious dinner!Keep up the good work you are doing. You bring joy to those who do not have much to look forward to. God bless you! Your lovely voice on the tape you gave me, will bless people in my country!

Once again, to Esther who took me to all the notable places, also to the Prayer Tower. How can anyone tell a stranger what happens during praise and worship there? Esther your companionship, love and endurance is something I cannot ever forget or even try to describe, how can I ever thank you enough. Just know, that God healed me, physically, and spiritually, during the more than four months I spent with you! GOD BLESS YOU! I am going back, and I am focused, to do God's will, all because of your love and compassion! You and Bruce will share in the fruit of your love and labor! Thanks for all the things I learned from you. Thanks for the food you made for me, and Bruce who provided it!.

Bruce, Thank you so much for your patience with an unenlightened lady. The computer was something awesome, just about awful, to me. Thank you for your help after all the blunders. Thank you for your computer I could use in writing this book. Had it not been for you, it would have been totally impossible. Please know that you have a lion's share in the results of this book! Thank you for your patience, in enduring me all the time there. God bless you with your very important work for your country!!

Chris, thank you for your help with the e-mails and the computer. Thank you for enduring discomfort all the time I spent there! I must have worn your patience very thin at times. Bless you, Michelle, for the presents you gave me! Carrie bless you too in your new life!

Bless Theo, the little doggy who gave me such love, joy and exercise, [and new glasses] he was my constant companion! I miss you. Thanks also to Jack, Eric, Jakes and the two Betty's, where Theo and I could rest and have water to drink during our walks. It was so good to have met you! Bless you!

If I left out somebody, please forgive me, just remember, I will think about each and every one back in South Africa, and I ask that God will bless and keep you! Regards to all! My life has been greatly enriched because of you all! If we do not meet here on earth again, look out for me in Heaven!

Mission Vision

Dear Reader. The desire to do more for the Master is burning higher than ever in my soul. I am now 68 plus years young, an ordained minister. By the grace of God, I am still healthy and strong, willing to go and to do what the Master tells me. I have written this book, about some of the extremely wonderful things I experienced in my walk with Jesus.

People are dying of Aids at a tremendous rate, in South Africa. If only we could be able to reach them with the Gospel before death takes it's toll!

I need to share with you what the Lord has told me. After my husband's death, I had to work to support myself. I was involved in an insurance business. One night I had a very clear dream from the Lord, in answer to my prayer to know if it was His will for me to be involved in the business.

In the dream a voice told me the following: "There are four stages to insurance. The first stage is when a person gets exposed to insurance. He or she then has to decide whether they need a funeral policy. What they decide in the first stage, determines what happens in the second stage. [This is true concerning all our decisions!]

I saw people driving around and heard them say: "We had better be very careful, because accidents do happen. Should something happen, our family will have to run around, trying to borrow money from the other family" I saw a second group driving around and heard them say: "We had better be very careful because accidents do happen, but fortunately, should something happen, we have made provision."

An extremely harsh, terrible, rasping, jarring, male voice said: "The third stage is when you really die!" It gave me the shivers!

Then I saw people going around trying to borrow money from family and friends. From my own experience, I know, death is traumatic enough, coupled to financial problems, it is just about unbearable.

In the forth stage, I saw people running around, trying to borrow money from family, for the funeral, or cremation.

Then a wonderfully beautiful, soothing voice said: **"But the beneficiaries will flock to you, saying:" "Thank you for talking to my Mom, or my Dad, or Aunt, or uncle** or whoever, for **provision has been made.** "

I woke up with a start, it was 2:10am. I said to the Lord, **"Lord, I would love to have a million beneficiaries** , but not for the insurance policy alone, **much more in the Kingdom of God."** I did not sleep again that night. I kept repeating, over and over that I would like to have a million beneficiaries, especially in the Kingdom of God!

This stayed in my mind, and every time I remembered, I repeated that I would love to have a million beneficiaries. About twelve days later I had the second dream. When God speaks to me, it is not in my own language, Afrikaans, it's much like the Dutch language, but He speaks to me in English.

The Lord said to me: **"You said that you would like to have a million beneficiaries?"**

I said **"Yes Lord, I would love** to have a million beneficiaries, **but as I told you,** not only in the insurance policy, **more so in the Kingdom'**

The Lord said to me: **"I will show you how you can have a million beneficiaries"** I laughed aloud, and said **"That I would really like to know how!"** The Lord said **"I want you to start, "ADOPT A PERSON INTERNATIONAL"**

I asked Him **"What does that involve, Lord?"**

He said to me **"All the Retirement Villages,** [the Old-age Homes in South Africa] **all the Apartments, all the Town Homes and even the homes are** full of lonely people, **and My People Sit In Church!"** **(I saw a very prim** and proper lady siting in a church, **and she** sounded like an American lady,) she said "Lord, { with a drawl} I would like to do something for you, but, I don't know what, I don't know how, and I don't know where!"

The Lord said:" Disciple-ship, has been taught and preached, for decades, but My people does not understand that at all. They are afraid I might send them to Russia, Nigeria or somewhere they do not want to go. Instead, **all they have to do, is to adopt one lonely person.** Find out their telephone number, call them, give them some love and understanding, (He then used a very down to earth word) **Find out what makes them TICK, and MY church will double in a month's time!"**

Dear reader, this is the message I have to deliver to as many ministries and Christians as possible. It was not born in MY spirit or in MY understanding. I have the obligation to share this revelation, what others do with it, is between them and the Lord. **God told me to start it.** Our responsibility is exclusively towards the Most High!I think **we should call it: "Each One Reach One!"**

Should you be interested to sow into our ministry, please contact me on my e-mail address, and I will give you a US Bank account number. I will also undertake to send you regular videos of what happens! **God Bless YOU,**

Rev, Finé Pienaar [Pronounced Finay]
E-Mail:**finepie@hotmail.com**

1

In the beginning God.... Looking back over the years, I realize more and more, that this is true concerning me, and I firmly believe, it is true in everybody else's life.

Let us look back together, only so will you be able to understand where I came from, and hopefully where I am heading! I grew up on a farm in the Orange Free State in South Africa. My parents actually wanted many more children, especially boys. It must have been a big disappointment when I, the third and last daughter made my appearance! My eldest sister was seven years older than the second, and she was eight years older than me.

By the time I was about four years old, both my sisters had left to go to school and university in town. My second eldest sister came home for a few weekends per school quarter. She always told me how spoilt I was. She teased me endlessly, plagued me, tickled and frightened me. Her presence did not make my life any more enjoyable. My eldest sister was a qualified teacher at that, time in a town far away. She got married when I was twelve years old. Therefore, I was alone and lonely all the time. My Mom had me when she was already forty- two.

My father was involved in many businesses, and a very difficult person to please. Oh boy, did he like a fight! He had law suites against many people, even against the government and railway department. It definitely did not make him very popular with the community, therefore, it made me unpopular as well.

Obviously I was very confused, because as a child I did not understand the things responsible for the bad attitudes towards me. I was only aware of the rejection from the other children at school, because their parents shared their bitterness with their children. I was only five and a half years old when I started attending school.

An old black man, went with me to school, he rode on a horse, and I on another naughty old horse. He had to wait for me at school, and came home with me after school. The school was about six miles from our home, quite a distance to go on horseback, especially when it was winter. The old horse, I rode on, knew and used all kinds of tricks. He caused me to be even more unpopular, by stealing the other children's lunches from their horse-carts, and because he kicked and bit their horses. When I was about eight years old, I wanted to prove that I could go to school on my own, because the children teased me, about my companion. I still rode on the very same old horse, but he now developed many new tricks.

My father stacked stones at each gate, on either side of the gate, because I was too small to get onto the horse by myself. On the way to, and from school, I had to open and close about eight gates. I would be struggling to get on the horse, from the stack, because he did not stand still. He would jerk his head up, and tear the reigns from my hands. Once free, he would start his mean campaign against me. He would start walking. If I walked behind him, he would walk, peeping over his shoulder to be sure that I followed. If I started to run, he would run. If I stopped, he stopped, and stared at me, over his shoulder. This process would be repeated over and over until we arrived home. I experienced this maddening desperation, time and time again!

Do you blame me that I kept crying, shouting, (not too pleasantly) talking and yelling at him. All to no avail, he usually had a great time, and enjoyed himself tremendously! Hatred raged in me, and frustration was always at the highest peak, because of the unbearably naughty old beast! Oh, he was responsible for many, many of my tears, frustration and suffering.

At school, when I wanted to saddle him, he would lift his head up so high, that I could not reach it to put the reigns over, or run away, that I couldn't catch him. When at long last, I had the reigns over his head, he would press his teeth together so hard, that it was impossible for me to get the bit in. I learned to kick him to distract his attention. Having secured the bridle he would try the next trick. He would keep moving, so I would not be able to put the heavy saddle on. When finally, I had the saddle on him, he would blow up his stomach, making it impossible for me to fasten the saddle belt. More kicks, as hard as possible, this time to his tummy, so that he had to breathe out, so I could fasten immediately. Eventually, the teacher had compassion on me, and helped me to catch and saddle him every day. I also tied a long piece of string to the bridle so, when he jerked his head up, I still had the string in my hand, to be able to force his head down. He seemed to sense when I was not concentrating very well, and he would immediately "indulge" in various lines of attack.

They say you can't teach an old horse any new tricks! Believe me, this one used both old, and new tricks each day. Because of the endless war, siege and struggle with this clever, mean old beast, and the teasing of the other kids, I refused to go to the farm school after grade five. I went to boarding school in our little town, with high hopes! I thought there would be no children who would make my life miserable because of my father. **I was proved wrong!**

he rejection was even worse. Coupled to this was my longing for my mother, the strange surroundings, and the food not always the way I liked. I had to clean my own room, make my own bed and see to my own clothes. I wasn't one of the popular pupils, and was still extremely lonely, shy and unhappy, with my self esteem even lower than before!

I am not sharing this with you, to have a pity party, but so that you can understand, you do not have to qualify for God to love or use you. The Bible, the precious Word of God tells us in" 1**Corinthians 1:26 Brothers (and sisters), think of what you were when you were called. Not many of you were wise by human standards; not many were influential; not many were of noble birth. 27. But God chose the foolish** things of the **world to shame the wise; God chose the WEAK things of the world to shame the strong. 28. He chose the LOWLY things** of this world **and the despised things** so that **no one may boast** before Him"

So, you do realize that I qualified, not because of my oppressive circumstances, but because of the love, favor and mercy of God. He saw my misery, my longings and weaknesses. Let us continue, because there are a lot of Stepping Stones, in the rest of the book. Once they were stumbling blocks, but Jesus changed them!

2

After grade seven, my parents realized that I was still not happy at school and decided to send me away to a very expensive, exclusive girl's school in a big town, far away from our little community, and all the prejudices against me.

Even though I still had a very low self-image and was shy, insecure and uncertain, nobody knew my father, so, for the first time in my life I had just myself to present and defend in the world. This was truly a new era, the ghost of my father was not there to make my life a misery. I was judged on my own standards, and free to grow into the person I wanted to become. I was happy, and had nice, unselfish friends, one was Mercia Wannenburg who is still one of my very special people. Thank you Mercia for having played such an important part in my life. She is the only friend I continued to see and enjoy after school.

After school I did not know precisely what I wanted to do. I decided to go back home to help my mother to care of my difficult old grandmother, till I knew what I wanted to do. My grand mother, really was very exacting and difficult to please. She had been staying with us for about 18 years, and because of her we never could go away on vacation. She was really not very grand, this grandmother! However all too soon I had a nice, rich young farmer friend, and study and work seemed to be of lesser importance.

One of my Aunts lived in a city about 200 miles from our farm. She provided board and food for people studying at the university. She had a special liking for one young man, and told him about her nice niece living on the farm. He became interested.

He wrote me a letter, telling me that he would like to meet me, and that he was staying with my aunt. Also that he hoped to become a minister in one of the three traditional Afrikaans churches. I had this nice rich farmer boyfriend, and wrote back that I had no real desire to meet him. The reason being, that I believed a preacher or a doctor was too much involved with their congregation, and patients, to be concerned enough with their family. However, he was not at all deterred or put off by that, he kept on writing such interesting letters that I began to enjoy the letters and looked forward hear from him. He asked for a photo of myself, well, I sent him one in a tree amongst so many leaves that only with the aid of a magnifying glass could you find my face.

He sent me a photo of himself. **wow**! Now, this definitely changed my attitude, he was very attractive and handsome! I then wanted to meet this guy. Well he came, he saw, I saw, and he conquered. It was love at first sight! I stayed on at the farm and less than a year later we were married. We moved into a small house, in the city, while he studied at the university. Our parents, on both sides, shared the cost of the rent and food. What a wonderful time we had!

He changed his study to BA. He then became an agnostic, because he said the students studying with him to become ministers of the Gospel, were the most undisciplined in the whole university. How could there possibly be a God if He would allow such undisciplined people to work for him? Drinking, smoking and doing much worse things. Unfortunately this happens very often. Instead of looking to God we look at the lives of other people, and make gross miscalculations, because of ignorance!

Well, he really did not study very hard! There were more important and pleasurable things to occupy us! Ignorance is not always bliss, believe me! Especially for me, I became pregnant immediately!!!

I was constantly sick. We did not at that time know that I had **rh neg** blood. It was extremely difficult, because I was nauseous, had back pain, my feet swelled and I was uncomfortable. Before the actual birth date, the gynecologist, decided to give me an induction to start the birth, because he feared that I might have kidney failure. I was a very long time in labor, despite the induction. My husband, being tired of the previous days of struggle, decided to go home to rest a while, and totally overslept! I was left alone to the dubious mercy of the nurses!

I begged them to call the gynecologist, but they would not, they said he was tired, he had delivered five babies the night before and needed the rest. I was totally alone and lonely, young , unenlightened, and could do nothing. They told me to hold back and not to work on the pains. When at last the gynecologist came, he told them to give me some chloroform, and again when he was putting on his surgical gloves. Our Elna had already suffered brain damage, but of course we only realized it much later.

When I got home with our baby, we received a letter from my father. He wanted us to come to live on the farm, because he wanted my husband to take over the farm. He wanted to retire, and go to live on his other farm. He said we would live together at first, just long enough, that he could teach my husband how to farm.

So, less than two weeks after Elna's birth, we moved to the farm in our very small Fiat Cub motorcar. The car had seats for two in front, with a small place for the new baby's crib in the back and hardly place for any luggage. My brother in law took all our earthly possessions in a small truck, including our two hens and a cock!

3

Our "NEW" life started. Wish I could tell you of big successes, unfortunately it was one great, colossal fiasco. Both my father and husband were very difficult, self-centered, men. Each of them, thought he alone knew best. Endless confrontations! There was NO peace at all. My father expected me to be loyal to him, but so did my husband. Soon I had serious nervous problems.

In all of this my dear mother had to try to keep the balance between all of us! She had to look after my grandmother, help my father with his other businesses, cook, clean, help me with the baby and see to all the other family who came to visit my grand mother! Not once did she have the wrong attitude, or was she impatient or short tempered. I really want to bring a tribute to the most wonderful mother who lived on earth. I do sincerely thank God for her, and not only for her, but also for all other real mothers.

She did not have the knowledge to lead me to the Lord, but the way she lived, proved that He was real to her. She sang Hymns and spiritual songs, was always sweet and patient, even under the most difficult situations. Whenever there was tough confrontations between my husband and father, she was ever impartial, and kept quiet.

This situation became unbearable, the tension never stopped, so my husband told my father that we were going to leave. There were more fights and arguments and finally my father decided to leave much sooner than he had expected, to live on his other farm. This caused many hard feelings and rifts, he told people that, figuratively speaking, he was undressing long before going to bed. He sold his farming machinery, his tractors and the other things we needed to be able to plant corn and wheat. Finally they left the farm, and we were left to cope as well as we could.

However, because of all the fights and problems we had, damage had been done to our relationship. Gone was the carefree, wonderful fun-filled time, the hard facts, the reality of life had to be faced, as best we could. We had to make a loan from the bank to enable us to farm. Everything seemed to be working against us. We had the one crop failure after the other. To plant corn, to see it grow beautifully until it had to form the cobs, and then to watch them wither, because of drought, that was to say the least, very traumatic. Or a few times we had some lovely wheat on the land, a most promising crop, and a cloud would come, from a total strange direction, to come to a standstill over our lands and have the hail remove every stalk of corn. We cried like babies. We were desperate, without hope and without God.

When our eldest daughter Elna was little over two years old, I became pregnant again. I promised the Lord, if it should be a boy that I would teach him about the Lord. Our eldest son Rian was born. He was the most beautiful baby I have ever seen. He had big blue eyes and golden curls. He developed very quickly. He could walk before he was nine months old, talk fluently, and he had to run away from his sister because she did not like him at all, and continually traumatized him. We then realized that she had brain damage, because she only started walking at nineteen months, she had difficulty talking and was much more difficult than Rian. But she could sing, dance, and keep a tune, before she could walk and talk, she received a wonderful gift from God!

arming was extremely difficult, rain often came too late and the banks would get impatient. We often were just about without hope. Because of all the stress I got asthma in a very bad way. No medication whatsoever helped at all. I was totally bedridden, sat in bed for twenty-four hours each day, suffocating and suffering. Because I was unable to do anything for my children or household, I felt totally useless and desperate. Nobody wanted to stay near me for very long, because I was having so much trouble breathing, it affected the visitors too much.

hen Rian was six months old I could stand the suffering no more. I called on God, and told Him that I did not want to live any longer, I meant nothing to anybody. I could not walk, talk or move because I had just enough oxygen to be able to survive barely.

y husband promised God (if there was a God) that he would serve Him, should He give me another chance and healed me. I told God that I did not want to live any longer, because I did not know about healing, by the Holy Spirit. I did not want to go to Hell, but did not know how to get to Heaven. I asked God to forgive me all my many sins, and tress-passes, and please to make it possible for me to go to Heaven. I had to accept that He did forgive me, I had no other option. Thereafter, I was like a plant. Quite resolved to die. No hope, no feelings, nothing to look forward to. I was totally without emotion, because if I became emotional I suffocated even more. Lonely in my suffering and rejected! I could not go on like that! Therefore, I decided that we needed to go to my in-laws to say my farewells. I did not know that God had an appointment with me there. His timing is always astoundingly perfect!

hen we got there, they were very excited. A visiting lady, so they heard, had a gift of healing from God, and they wanted me to go to see her. I couldn't care, and didn't care, whether we went or whether we stayed. I was ready to depart from earth, nothing at all mattered. So just to please them, I succumbed to their pressure, and said I would go. BUT GOD wasn't through with me yet!

The next day we went to see this lady, she prayed for me. She told me I had catarrh as well as asthma, in a very advanced stage, but nothing is impossible with God. I came away feeling very, very much better. The day after, I went to see her again, and I was totally healed!

After all the months of suffocating, smothering, suffering and agony, trying to force a little air into my lungs, I could breathe freely. Praise the Lord! Our snobbish, learned friends would never accept that God had healed me supernaturally, but I was there, at deaths door, and knew better. A miracle does help to make you realize that there are more things than meets the eye, but it does not save your soul. Only the miracle cleansing blood of Jesus does that. I still had to experience that, even though I testified that God healed me!

Having been so lonely when I grew up, I wanted more children. However, I could not become pregnant again. I tried and tried, but to no avail. The doctors said it seemed that I would not have any more children. After more than five years, I fell pregnant again. My joy was boundless! I decided to make absolutely sure that nothing would go wrong.

We were driving at a high speed, on a highway, when I saw a car standing at a side-road, I suddenly had a premonition. I said to Peter, beware of that car! The lady didn't see us and pulled away, she struck our car on my door. The blow sent us flying off the road, directly towards a big, big iron corner pole. I grabbed the wheel with Peter, in an endeavor to keep it from striking the pole. We missed it by inches, we came to a standstill next to the pole, in the fence. The car had "flown' through the air more than thirty yards, When the police came, they said several cars has had an accident there, we were the first ever, not to die, because of the big iron corner pole! Peter asked me to take the wheel of the car to have it towed out. Well, Peter and I thought we did a good job, steering the car away from the pole. Imagine the fright I got when I tried to steer the wheel of the car, it was totally loose! The steering rod was broken! God, not our efforts, saved our lives! Also the life of my unborn baby!

The desire to prevent anything wrong to happen when the baby had to be born, caused me a lot of anxiety. After a false alarm, and an induction that did not work, I asked the Lord when my baby would be born. I opened the Bible and read that Jesus came to Jerusalem six days before the feast. I knew it could not be six days Christmas, since that was too late in December, I realized it had to be the tenth, six days before another special day of remembrance in South Africa.

When the contractions started, the afternoon of the tenth, my husband ran out to check if everything was in order with the car. He shouted from outside "Come help me, I have broken my leg!" When I got to him he was lying on the ground. Not his leg was broken, but he had severed the Achilles' tendon above his heel. His foot was absolutely limp, but the calf-muscle jerked up and down, up and down! It looked extremely strange, and ludicrous!

This was a very real problem! I was in labor, and he had to go to hospital! Without me knowing about it, he had been using a drug, advertised as guaranteed harmless, for slimming. It had to be taken in the morning to enhance your energy, but he had been taking it in the evenings when I was sleeping. He then had a "high" like with drugs, and got totally addicted. This "HIGH" could not be detected, it had no smell like alcohol or marijuana. This drug caused all his muscles and tendons to become brittle like dried meat, jerky in the USA, called biltong in South Africa. He had taken another dose just before I told him that I had to go to the maternity hospital. He was already "high," that was why he ran outside! Catastrophe!

His foot was so limp, I bound it to planks in the form of a right mark. I had to drive the car, since he had no control of his foot. Between contractions I drove at a terrific speed, slowing down, and down, when pain hit me. He was in a state of shock, saying "You must rush, I cannot drive, and I cannot catch the baby either. Hurry, Hurry!" The town we were going to, was thirty-two miles away from our farm. We got to our friend's home at ten past midnight! I had told her about the scripture, so she was still up and waiting for us to come. We left our two children with her, then our friend took our car, drove my husband to hospital, and took me to the maternity hospital. OH! I was so alone and lonely! And frightened!

As soon as I was in the hospital, I realized that I forgot to warn the nursing staff at the other hospital about Peter's deadly allergy to morphine. I wanted to use the telephone, but had no money for the pay phone. The Sister on night duty, was just as unhelpful and unfriendly as the one at Elna's birth. Our enemy, the Devil, always tries the same tactics that worked previously.

I prayed all night for Peter. I was extremely worried, I knew if he died that night, he would definitely not go to heaven, but to the wrong place! I also implored, begged, and pleaded with the nurse to call my doctor. I knew if he came, he could call the hospital where Peter was, and he could also visit him. It all fell on deaf ears. She blatantly refused to call the doctor!

At half past five, I rang the bell to I call the nurse once more, I told her I was going to deliver the baby in the bed. She would not believe me, but I told her to take a look, and examine me. After peeping, she used very strong words, darted out of the room, returned with the trolley, rolled me onto it, and ran to the delivery room. She called the doctor and told him to come quickly! Five minutes later my precious daughter, Carise, was born, also without a doctor!.

The after effects of all the stress and anxiety, caused my arms, legs and all my body to jerk and jump involuntarily, unrestrainedly in all directions. I could not control any part of my body, it felt as though I was being torn apart.

When the doctor came, he looked at me, and was very concerned about me. He wanted to know what was going on, why was I jerking like that? I told him the nurse bluntly, blatantly refused to call him, all night long. I told him what had happened to Peter, and that I had to take him to hospital. I told him she did not want to call the hospital to warn them about him being allergic to morphine, and about my worry over him. All the while I was jerking and crying. —I kind of think, if ever, I had the right to be emotional, it surely was that morning!

Thank God, Oh! SO Very much! I did not have another mentally retarded child because of somebody else's negligence, and spitefulness. She is the most precious gift any mother could ever have received!

Because I told the doctor about the nurse's behavior, it was as though I had a contagious disease, the nurses treated my very coldly. So, the next day I released myself from hospital, I called my friend to fetch me, and went to their home. I left my baby at there, and went to see Peter. I heard the horrible truth: The nurse, without asking him, if he was allergic, had given him a double dose of morphine—"so that he could rest well!" HA! HA!

Of course, the antihistamine of the slimming-pill, produces energy, and worked against the morphine, that is a depressant! This caused his lungs to collapse, so that he barely stayed alive. Instead of resting, he had to fight for his life, all night long. The next day before the operation, the specialist tested him for allergic responses to narcotics. Every one immediately caused a sore on his skin! They had to use the one with the least negative reaction, to put him to sleep for the operation.

The specialist told him that they could not guarantee the success of the operation. Sinews and tendons do not fuse and grow together, like muscles or bones. They had to stitch the muscle through and through with gut, like when you darn a sock. He had to remain in a plaster cast for three months, his foot, as well as his whole leg, to give the sinew a reasonable chance to grow together. Thereafter he was always aware of the weakness of this tendon. The specialist told him, if it should break again, nothing at all could be done to mend it.

The breathing problem he got because of the morphine and the drug working against each other, became part of the rest of his life. Young people use ecstasy and other related drugs very carelessly. All these drugs have the same after- effects as those he suffered. OH! I wish I could warn all people!

Peter also had problems with depression and was unable to go to sleep. The Bible states clearly: Rom 6:23 "For the wages of sin is death, but the gift of God is eternal life in Christ Jesus our Lord." Therefore, the wages of the sin he committed had a very bad effect, and made him suffer. God forgave him, gave him eternal life, but the devastation in his body remained. I could never find out, if it was through lack of faith, or what the reason was. I only know that he loved the Lord with all his heart!

I sincerely hope it will warn someone to stop using drugs, or to keep them from starting. Turn to Jesus for eternal life, have your wages changed! The Devil's wages are devastation. He is a murderer from the beginning! Jesus is the only merciful paymaster! His wages are good beyond description! **PSM. 103. 10 He has not dealt with us after our sins, nor rewarded us according to our iniquities. (Now one of my favorite Bible texts.) 11.For as the heavens are high above the earth, so great are His mercy and loving-kindness, toward those who reverently and worship-fully fear Him.**

4

We were still struggling on the farm, trying to eke out an existence. I had some Jersey cows, and had raised a beautiful bull. Unfortunately this bull was very aggressive, he only listened to me and two of the black men who fed him from the time he was a small calf. One Sunday, on Peter's birthday, the servants did not close the gate properly, so Ferrus, the bull, came and walked all round our home. The children wanted to play outside the house, but couldn't, because of the dangerous bull.

I wanted Peter to take the car to call the black man to take the bull away, but he started playing with him over the wall. I warned him, but men usually do what they want, and he stroked the big bull's head, and talked to him. The bull, of course, enjoyed the attention for as long as it suited him. Then Peter started chasing him away, and very docilely he walked on, watching all the time over his shoulder whether Peter was following. He walked on steadily, till he realized he had enticed Peter far enough from the house.

He swung around like lightning and charged! Peter could maybe have made it back to the house, but he was only three weeks out of the cast, learning to walk again, his foot was still limp, unsteady and unsure!

When the bull got to him, he grasped his horns, but with brute strength he pushed Peter over! He tried to use his horns like swords, to pierce him, but Peter managed to dodge them. The bull then knelt, and tried to kneel on top of Peter! He pushed with all his might, Peter could hear his ribs break, the one after the other, ONE, TWO, THREE!

I was preparing his birthday lunch in the kitchen, when a black lady came running in to tell me that the bull was killing my husband! I ran out with only a kitchen towel in my hands. I saw the bull on top of Peter! I pushed his head away, and shouted his name FERRUS! Because he knew me, he budged! Peter rolled out and we both ran for the house. Because he was down, the bull could not get up soon enough to attack again!

There is always something amusing in every situation, if we are willing to look for it. Peter ran to the house, thanks to the adrenaline rush! Once inside though, he was totally cripple! He could not walk unaided. It was very funny! He definitely did not appreciate my amusement then!

We had no birthday lunch, because we went to the hospital, where the x-rays showed the three broken ribs, and he saw the specialist for his foot. Fortunately the tendon was not torn, but he had to use crutches again. The ribs, however, took a long and painful time to heal. God had spared his life again!

Less than a month later, Peter was fixing the electric wiring in the roof of an outbuilding. He had switched off the power, but somehow the power came on. His head was against the tin roof, to steady him, so the full 220 current, passed through him. Fortunately it threw him off the ladder, otherwise he would have been electrocuted. He fell about thirty feet to the ground, hurt his ribs again, but because he was limp from the electric shock, did not break anything else, though every part of his body was sore! He was unconscious from the shock and fall. He woke up, thinking he was dead or something, because about ten black faces were bent over and staring at him! Once more God had intervened to spare his life!

When Carise, our second daughter, was three, our son Karel was born. Fortunately I suffered no ill affects during pregnancy, and this time Peter was also with me at the time of his birth. Karel, was a difficult baby, he knew from the beginning precisely what he wanted. He was about two years old, when one night he asked for water, he said: "I want water in a plastic glass, Please."

I usually got what the children wanted, but did not feel well that night, because I had flue. I asked to get the water in the plastic glass, please, but he brought it in a glass, glass. Karel, would not accept the water, he said he did say, he wanted it in a PLASTIC glass, and he DID say PLEASE! After the third spanking, I got up to fetch him water in a plastic glass. It is a very good characteristic, it has helped him to excel at school and in his work. Though, sometimes it causes us to expect too much, even of ourselves.

At that stage, we were still struggling on the farm, and it did not go well with our marriage. Peter should not have tried to farm, because his interests were in totally different things. He was very, very clever and talented, and should have been a developer of industrial patents. He had amazing ideas, but as usual with a developer, once the thing worked, he lost interest. It needed someone with marketing skills to take it further, and we did not have the right persons for that.

Well, they say opposites attract each other. Unfortunately physical attraction, is not enough in a relationship. Because he was frustrated, he often took out his frustration on me, and our kids. Once he gave me another blue eye, a third, a painful one! Later, I told him, that if ever again in his life, he lifted his hand to beat me, he would never be able to sleep peacefully, ever after! He wanted to know, what I meant by that? I told him very clearly, I was not to be used as a boxing sack. If he ever did hit me again, he would never know which night I would get back at him with a knife! I have seen this phenomena in so many other relationships too.

He was more interested in Chess, chess books and all kinds of difficult subjects. He never wanted to visit other people, except, if they were chess or bridge players, or could argue about philosophy. He used to say he had nothing to tell anyone, all he knew he got out of books. Should they want to know anything, they could find the information, the way he got it, by reading.

This reading and searching for truth and reality can get us into the wrong kind of things. He found books about astral projection in the library. This caused him to try practicing all of those things. It scared me overmuch, and I did not want to have any part in that. I always told him that, when he went out of his body, he had no guarantee that a wrong spirit might not enter. Later, when he was so extremely difficult to live with, I thought that it really might have happened! So many people are lead astray through lack of knowledge: Hosea 4.6 "My people are destroyed from lack of knowledge" The Bible is the ONLY pure source of truth and knowledge.

Maybe, someone reading this is also at the end of his, or her patience, power, hope and desire to continue, please do not stop reading! There are much, much better things to come! But, please keep in mind, God is waiting for your call, His line is never busy, you may call anytime! Call the heavenly number. This is it: **Jeremia. 33.3 "Call to Me and I will answer you and show you great and mighty things, fenced in and hidden, which you do not know** do not distinguish and recognize, have knowledge of and understand."

I had an ever growing desire to get to know the Lord, but Peter was just the opposite. During November 1965 I told my mother, that I was planning to leave Peter, there was just nothing left between us anymore. She admonished me, and told me to try one more time, she promised she would pray very earnestly for us.

In the beginning of January 1966, I was fed-up! I had it! I wanted out! I wanted to quit! In my desperation, I decided to go to the Lord one more time, concerning Peter, and our marriage. Even though I did it so many times before. (It always is the best place to go!) I told the Lord, that I was tired of trying to make our marriage work. It was totally one-sided, all effort came from me. And I told the Lord that I was sure, if he, Peter, could be sure, and know that God really IS, it would change him. (I did not know about being born again, or how to become a child of God) Then I asked the Lord to tell me, IF Peter would know sometime, and be sure that God exists, how long would it be before he knew? I said please, Lord, let it not be LONG. My spiritual strength was about gone. Speak to me from the Bible and tell me how long it will be, before he will undoubtedly know, about You, Lord that You are real?

I opened the Bible, I saw as a part of a verse, in the right hand column of the left page, just about in the middle of the page. Please, I want you to realize, I remember even where it was written! It made an indelible impact on me! I read:

"Within the first three months of the year, he will know!" Oh! **What Joy!** What a tremendous relief! **What a precious promise!** Hope flooded my soul! There was something to hold onto. **God cannot lie!**

Never, ever, again did I find that scripture! However, the supernatural things that happened thereafter, proved that I did receive that promise, in answer to my call. Our Amazing, Wonderful, Loving God did hear, did heed, and did answer, My desperate call. If you are desperate, just call on Him!

5

The promise, did not make a saint of me overnight! We still had fights, and arguments, but I would suddenly realize and remember! The PROMISE! I would then tell him: "OH! Just forget about it! Everything will be different in three months time!" He would then get even more cross, wanting to know from me, what this three months story was all about!?

The last week in March 1966, we were visiting with friends in Pretoria. They were lovely people, they did not swear, smoke, drink liquor, or went to wrong places. But, they neglected, to testify about the Lord. I sensed that they had a relationship with the Lord, so I always asked them to pray for Peter, to come to know the Lord.

t was the thirty first of March! The end of the first three months! Nothing had happened yet! I went to bed, while Peter was still talking to Mike, our friend. In our bedroom, I told the Lord, that the three months were over. There was just the night left. I said, I could call Peter to tell him that God does exist. I had done that so many times in the past, but it had made NO impact or difference. So, I had to trust Him to talk to Peter, so that He would understand! I went to sleep, and did not know what time Peter came to bed.

At about three o'clock Peter woke me! HE WAS WEEPING! This hard hearted Peter, was actually weeping! He said to me, that the Lord had spoken to him. He had been trying in his own way to ascertain if there was a God. But, he always had provisions, if, the Lord healed him, he would serve the Lord. IF the Lord healed me, he would serve the Lord. If this, and if that!

Then the Lord spoke to him and said: "You have always said to Me, IF I heal you, you would serve Me. Now I am asking you, If I heal you what are you going to do?" THIS WAS THE LORD!

23

All the stress, the tight, strangling grip on his throat, his difficulty with breathing. It ALL disappeared! Immediately he was free! Free, Totally free! —Without a shadow of a doubt, he KNEW GOD SPOKE to him! When God, in His Wonderful Love and Authority speaks to us, we KNOW that it is GOD! How precious to KNOW that there is more to life than just to eat and rink, and then die. There is One who cares about us! Someone WHO loves us! Someone, Who knows all, and will lead us.

After he shared this with me, I told him, I want to wake Mike and Santa to tell them the GOOD NEWS! I told him, that they would be extremely glad to hear that God had spoken to him. He wanted to stop me, but I rushed past him. I wanted to have witnesses to what had happened. In the past, he also woke me, when his conscience bothered him. Then he would tell me we should change our lives, but the next morning, he would tell me he had just been overwrought, and over-tired!

When I woke them, Mike and Santa were very glad to hear the Good News! We all wept with joy! They said we should pray together, to thank the Lord! They did most of the praying, because I was so over-joyed, I could hardly speak! After prayer, I went to the bedroom, and Peter to the restroom.

Peter always said, **he had very humble beginnings.** He was on the toilet, thinking about what had happened, when the Enemy talked to him, and tried the old trick that had worked for so many years! OH! He was just overtired, worried and overwrought! He had a problem! Now, we would all think that he was religious like us! How would he be able top escape?

Suddenly, Peter realized that he was at **the most crucial time of his whole life!** It felt so good to believe, it was wonderful to be able to believe that God knew about him, and had a plan for him. If he could not believe at that moment, how would it be possible ever again to believe? With desperate urgency, he called on God to help him! For the second time, **in His condescending mercy, God spoke to him!** He said to **Peter:"Go to your room there is a message for you in the Bible"**

I waited for Peter, my heart overflowing with gratitude. Gratitude that God kept His promise. Gratitude, that He spoke to Peter. Gratitude that there would be a better life ahead. Of a sudden, I wanted to know what God would say to him from the Bible. I asked God to give me a scripture for him. I opened the Bible and I read:

Luke.15.7 Thus, I tell you, there will be more joy in heaven over one (especially) wicked person who repents (that is,) changes his mind, abhorring his errors, and misdeeds, and determines to enter upon a better course of life than over ninety-nine righteous persons who have no need of repentance.

When Peter in agony of mind and spirit, rushed into the room, I said to him: "Here is YOUR scripture verse from the Bible!" He reeled! It was too real! Gone were the negative input from the Devil!!

He went to sleep, because he did not have the usual trauma! I could not sleep for joy! I got up long before Peter, because I had to tend to our kids. I did not know what to expect from Peter. So, I told Santa, if Peter got up, saying that it was just tiredness, and that he was overwrought, I would leave him. [Definitely not faith inspired words!] She was worried, and said we should pray!

Peter came out of the bedroom, with his burning cigarette, looking morose and unfriendly! He went straight to the restroom! He did not have much sleep the previous night, and he was unused to wake up with the Lord. He was on the toilet again, when suddenly the whole agenda played in his mind! He must have been more tired and overwrought than usual, it must have been all a lot of coincidences! How would he be able to get out of it this time? And then, the Holy Spirit did His work again. On the other hand, he had to admit, it felt very good to be able to believe. But he did not believe now! **He cried out to God and asked** HIM: **"What must I do to be able to all the time to believe, that You do exist?** That was when he said to the Lord; **"Please speak to me from this Woman' Magazine,** and tell me what I have to do, to be able always to believe. It is too hard, one moment to be able to believe, and then not to believe."

I said to Santa, it really did not look too good, or promising! We continued to pray, rather she continued! While she was praying, he came out of the restroom, very excited! The same man, who formerly told me, that I tempted God to ask for a scripture, came to show us, what God gave him from a woman's magazine! I will have difficulty to interpret, because it used typically South African expressions, but I will try my best! This is the interpretation!

"You will have to bite hard and firmly and bite through, and hold on with your teeth, for it will take tenacity and perseverance, but only thus, will you become a happy and successful MAN!

How could that come from a Woman's magazine? The article was about newly weds. The husband should be willing to adopt and adept to his new wife's ways, because she might not do precisely as his Mom used to do. However to a Christian it is a spot-on message. We need tenacity and perseverance in all of our daily living, all the way!

How exceedingly wonderful, to know, that magazine was printed nearly a thousand miles away. It had to be brought to Pretoria, my friend had to buy it, and then place it in the toilet! It needed to be there for Peter to ask a message out of it, when he was in dire need.

The enemy was gone again, with this precious admonition! However, it takes time for a baby to grow big and strong enough to start walking! How much more do we have to exert patience, first with ourselves, and with every other baby or young Christian too!

6

Hope flooded my soul! What great things to envision for a better, hopeful future! I would be able to endure hardship, should there be hope of **better things, just three months away!** It was a total reality in my mind! The Almighty God, cannot and will not lie! In more than thirty-five years thereafter, I have never again found that scripture! But, what happened proved that it was right and true! It was truly meant for me!

Unfortunately, that **hope did not make me a saint,** we still had arguments and fights, but in the midst of those I would suddenly remember! **Within three months!** I would stop arguing, saying to him: "Don't worry, just forget about the argument, within three months, everything will be different!" It used to rattle and make him even more aggressive, he asked me time and time again: "What is this you know about this three months story, that is going to change everything?" Of course, I could not tell him, I would say, oh, just leave it at that, it shall be sorted out.

January and February went by, so did more than half of March. The last week of March, we went to Pretoria, about 200 miles from our farm. Peter was busy registering some patents. We stayed with friends, Mike and Santa, while we were there. Eventually the thirty first of March arrived! The three months was past!

That evening, Peter was busy talking to our friend, and I went upstairs to our bedroom. I said to the Lord: "This is the last day of the first three months, there is only this night left. I can call Peter now, and tell him, that You, Lord, do exist. I have done that many times in our lives, but it made **No difference.** However, I **do believe, that You Lord, will do what You promised,** please reveal Yourself to him." I do not know what time he came to bed, because I fell asleep.

At about three o'clock, Peter woke me, he was crying! This hard man was actually weeping! He told me that God had spoken to him.

God said to him: "Peter you a always try to reason, to find out if I do exist. You always have conditions and bargains, and try to make a deal with Me." **"Lord, If You do this, then I will do that!"** God asked him: "You always said to Me, If I should heal you, you would serve Me. Tonight I am asking you, if I heal you, what will you do?" Undeniably, **if God** in His infinite wisdom and love **chooses to communicate** with us humans, there is NO gainsaying! **We KNOW that it is God!**

Beloved reader, all his stress, breathing problems, with something strangling him all the time, fell away! Then he woke me, and told me about his experience.

You can be sure that I was overjoyed! God kept His promise! It was tremendously wonderful! The realization that God does care about me, cared enough to make a promise, but also to keep the promise! **What Joy!**

In times past, Peter had often told me that we should change and rectify our lifestyle. This had always happened when his conscience bothered him. However, the next morning he would tell me that he had been strained, tired or overwrought! And I just had to forget about it!

I never had a witness to his confessions, hence, I could not pass up the opportunity to have two witnesses! I told him, that I wanted to tell our friends that God had spoken to him, they would be very glad to hear about it! He tried to discourage and stop me, but I slipped past him and woke them.

When they heard what had happened, they were exceedingly glad! They said we should pray and thank God. Well, they prayed, and thanked God. Peter and I wept and rejoiced silently. My heart was really overflowing with thankfulness. I did not have words strong enough to express my feelings! Eventually, I went to our bedroom,

Peter to the toilet. As always, in great joy, great need or pain, I asked the Lord to talk to me from the Bible.

I opened the Bible and read: the **Luke 15.4 "Suppose one of you has a hundred sheep and loses one of them. Does he not leave the ninety-nine and go after the lost sheep till he finds it? 5. And when he finds it, he joyfully puts it on his shoulders and goes home. 7 tell you there will be more rejoicing in heaven over one sinner who repents"** It was such a perfect description of Peter, I could not help but weep and rejoice and wait for him to return from the toilet! He always said that he had very humble beginnings!

While he was on the toilet, all this was so new to him, that God had spoken to him! Then the enemy of our souls spoke to him too. In times past it had always worked. "Peter you are overtired, stressed and overwrought, it was emotional stress that caused you to believe that God spoke to you! It was just your imagination!" He suddenly had to choose which voice to believe. **Oh! The unfathomable riches of God's love and mercy! He spoke to Peter for a second time,** in his confusion about the different voices. God said: **"Go to your room, there is a message for you in the Bible"** He literally ran to our room!

As he opened the door, **I said to him: "Here is your message from the Bible!"** I saw him reel, as if he had received a blow, it was too real! He read the message, and back was his joy!

The magnitude of what had happened to Peter, kept me awake, and I got up long before him. I did not know what his reactions would be, whether he would ascribe all to the state of his mind again. I said to my friend Santa: "I have waited long enough, I want to serve the Lord, and if Peter has other plans, I am going to leave him." Definitely the words and works of the flesh! She intervened, she said let us pray now! She switched on her hair drier in order to dull the sound of our prayers.

We were still praying, when Peter came out of our room, a cigarette in his hand, looking glum. (glum, meaning: moody and silent, sullen!)- **He went into the toilet!** Not at all encouraging! My friend asked the Lord's help, urgently, immediately!

Suddenly Peter rushed into the room! **He was so excited he could barely talk!** This is what happened!

He was on the toilet, (humble beginnings) not feeling well after a night with very little sleep, and lots of emotional ups and downs. He sat smoking and leafing through a woman's magazine, when **suddenly! He remembered! Something happened** the night before! **God spoke to him! Or did He?** —He was in the same devastating turmoil! —Wasn't he just tired and overwrought? —Or was it his imagination? Maybe it was just pure coincidence! —What if it were, and we wanted him to believe the same things we believed?

Then he realized he was at the most crucial point in his whole life! It was so easy to believe the night before, if he did not use the opportunity now, **maybe he would never be able to believe!** In his heart **he called on God!** He said: **"Lord, this is very difficult! One moment I do believe, the next I don't** believe! This is much harder than just not to believe all the time! **What must I do to be able to believe at all times?"**

his now was the man who always told me that I was "tempting" God, when I asked for a word from God in the Bible, even though he questioned God's existence. This same man, now, in his agony, asked God for a word in a Woman's magazine! **Rom 12.33 O the depth of the riches and wisdom and knowledge of God! And how untraceable (mysterious, undiscoverable) are His ways—His methods, His paths.**

This book was printed a thousand kilometers away! My friend had to buy it, place it in the restroom, for Peter to be able to ask a word from it! The word when he opened it, was SPOTON! It is exceedingly difficult to interpret from Afrikaans into English, but I will try my best.

He read: "You will have to gnash your teeth, by biting hard and by biting thoroughly, and holding onto it real fast, and it will take tenacity and perseverance, but only by doing that, will you become a happy and successful MAN!"

That from an exclusively woman's magazine! We rejoiced, because it was exactly right. It still is the only way to become a successful man, or also a successful woman! Later we read the article, it was concerning a newly wed man, should the new wife not cook or do the way Mom used to! He then, would have to learn to endure and be patient.

Surely, that hit the doubt for a home run! However, we cannot collect manna for many days, we have to have fresh faith for now!: Hebr.11.1 Now, Faith is the assurance of the things we hope for, being the proof of things we do not see faith perceiving as real fact what is not revealed to the senses.

7

Our friends were extremely glad about what had happened, and we were encouraged spiritually. They told us that we could stay in their house to conclude my husband's business concerning the patents, but they had to go away for the week, to be spiritually charged and renewed. Well! That sounded exactly what we needed, I told her that. They were very excited at first and said that they would arrange for lodging, food and all we needed. So the next night was my turn to be sleepless.

We had planted beans when the corn died of drought, but the beans died too. Peter and everybody else told me that there was no chance whatsoever of beans being resurrected and revived, even if we had rain. I told them that God could still do wonders, He had healed me from asthma, and He could make the beans grow again. They told me clearly and in a very condescending way, that I was way out to believe that.

In answer to my fervent prayers it did rain, the beans in contradiction to what they had said, was resurrected! They grew so well and were bearing extremely well. The question now was, should we go to the conference or not? The beans should to be harvested before it became dry, because then they could spill out of the pods. We needed the money more than desperately, and could not risk loosing the crop, but I had to know God's will!

I lied awake, wanting to know what we should do, Conference or beans. I asked God to tell me, and give me the solution. Suddenly, dear reader a heavenly smell enveloped me! You can be sure of this: Heaven is a sweet smelling place, remember, in Heaven the roses never fade. It was the most beautiful fragrance I ever smelled. I had goose-bumps all over my body. I sensed the awesome presence of the Lord. He spoke to me very clearly and asked:

"What did Abraham answer Isaac when he asked him, "See, here are the fire and the wood, but where is the lamb for a burnt sacrifice?" I knew the answer to the question: "God himself will provide" —I knew without a shadow of a doubt that we had to go to the conference!

Our friends were afraid that we would not understand what was going on at their conference. I asked if they did anything obscene. They were horrified at my question, oh no they do nothing wrong, but they pray very loud and long, and maybe we will be scared by that. In my ignorance I said to her, no, we would definitely not be offended by the way they prayed. Had I but known! I believe God watches us, and are many, many times superbly amused at all we do, and say!.

We arrived at about four-thirty, when the afternoon service was just finishing. Well, they were praying much harder and louder than I had ever heard. We were offended! My husband and I glanced at each other, what on earth was going on here? This had to be the "sects" we were warned about. How could we possibly escape? We did not want to hurt our friends, but this was more, much more than we bargained for. Anyway, the kids were tired after the long journey, all of us were tired and hungry, so the best would be to wait until everyone was asleep, and then to make a run for it.

We all bathed, had supper and went to bed, wanting to go as soon as they were asleep! Remember how God put Adam to sleep, to remove a rib to make Eve? That's about how fast we slept that night. Even the four children did not stir. Our friends had to wake us up, because we were already late for breakfast, we totally overslept. The first meeting was already over. No chance to flee, and no place to hide.

At ten o'clock we went to the second meeting, it was totally strange to us. See, we only went to church for our babies to be dedicated, sprinkled (not baptized), for weddings and funerals. The ladies sat on one side, the men on the other side of the hall. The people sang as though they really meant what they sang. The message was a strong call for dedication to the Lord, the invitation at the end impressed us with the urgency to accept the Lord. All this was new, we had never experienced that kind of dedication to the Lord. Well, we stayed. We saw the earnestness and sincerity of all the people, they really meant business with the Lord. We heard testimonies of people being healed, **we heard of wonderful answers to prayer** and many encouraging spiritual happenings.

We went to every meeting, and I asked everyone to pray for my husband. Fortunately, they must have realized that I needed prayer too. I heard for the first time that **you have to accept the Lord Jesus as your personal savior, to become a child of God. I did that, the first time I heard the good news.**

Come Saturday-night, I was already a bit uptight, my husband had not given any sign that he was convinced about accepting the Lord. That night the preacher preached on Peter, who had to let go of the boat, when Jesus, walking on the water, told him to step out and come to him. My husband went out for prayer after the invitation. **I thought my heart would burst with joy!** I kept thinking: "A new life, Lord Jesus, a new life with you!" The elders prayed with him for a long time, I suppose he had a lot of questions, but there was a definite breakthrough. **He did accept the Lord as his personal Savior!**

We spent the rest of the evening listening to wonderful testimonies. Eventually when we got to our bedroom, I asked him very cautiously if we could pray together. Oh! My! My ego got quite a bit bashed. I had always read the Bible, I had always prayed, I had always believed, I had always wanted to find God's will, and here now was my husband getting revelation upon revelation. He told me many things, and we kept talking so he did not go to sleep till after one o'clock.

I could not sleep. My heart was too much to full to sleep. I wanted to work for the Lord, I thought about the lady where I was healed from asthma, and said I would also like to have the gift of healing, or I was prepared to work in any way God wanted me to. I had no supper the night before, but suddenly felt my belly getting fuller and fuller. I said: "Lord, I did not even eat last night, why am I getting fuller and fuller?"

Suddenly I felt my tongue starting to twist in my mouth, I wanted to make strange sounds. I said: "What is this now?" The Devil talked loudly and said: "This is just bugs" In my ignorance I thought it was my sins getting out, (my husband later said I must have thought that my sins would percolate out.) The Lord said to me "This is the gift of the Holy Spirit, and it is the strange tongues spoken of in 1 Cor. 14" He went on to tell me that He wanted ME to go to Uncle Sakkie, (I will not mention the surnames) and Marinda, before the seven o'clock prayer meeting. I knew that I had to touch them with my hands and pray for them! But who are they, and what is wrong with them? How will I be able to pray for them?

My mother taught me to pray till I was six years old, but no one ever after that had asked me to pray. What will I say to them, why do I want to pray for them? What will I answer should they ask me questions?

I wrestled with many more questions, to such an extent that I could not go to the prayer meeting. Eventually we were in the 10 o'clock meeting. **God said to me: "You say you want to work for Me, but, you are not willing to do the first task I ask you to do!"** I cried and cried. My heart felt like breaking, I was totally devastated. I heard nothing of the sermon that morning.

After the meeting we went to eat. When I had dished up for my kids, I sat down with a plate of delicious food. I looked at the food, I had not eaten since the previous midday meal, and could not eat. It kept ringing in my ears: **"Go Now! Go Now! Go Now!"** I asked permission to leave.

Instead of going to look for those two strangers whose names the Lord had given me, I went to our bedroom. I took my Bible, and I told the Lord that I could not fathom or understand how He could have picked me, to give me the gift of the Holy Spirit. I thought I was the only person to have received the gift, because I had never heard about anybody else. I said to Him, why did my mother not receive it, she was a much, much better person than I. Would he please tell me why I received the gift? I took my Bible and opened it, I read:

Matt: 7:11."If you, then, though you are evil, know how to give good gifts to your children, how much more will your Father in heaven give good gifts to those who ask him!" I had my answer, had I not asked the Lord to use me, as he had used the lady who prayed for me?

I humbly thanked the Lord for the gift, however, the knowledge that He wanted to give it to me, did not make it clear how I should use it. I then went in search for the two people I did not know, neither did I know what the matter were with them. The time I spent in our bedroom praying was about fifteen minutes.

Everybody was still eating lunch, then I saw a lady, and I went to her and asked where I could find uncle Sakkie. She told me that he got so sick, that they had left for home ten minutes earlier. Oh I felt terrible! What if he died on the way home? Maybe he would not go to heaven and I could have prevented that! I then asked her where I could find Marinda. She told me that it was her daughter. I asked her if I could pray for her, but she said Marinda was still eating, and it would be best if I would always remember to pray for her. I was an outsider, a stranger, using make-up, so, they did not believe that my prayers would amount to much. **How often do we judge the book by its cover?**

I walked away, **I said "Mission uncompleted, Lord"** You can't imagine how bad I felt. Well, about a month later I had the privilege to pray for uncle Sakkie, he had been suffering for more than ten years of a strange kind of sickness, God healed him immediately. Unfortunately it did not go so well with **Marinda. She had polio** as a child, therefore her feet were deformed, and **because her mother did not allow me to pray for her, she stayed that way.**

How often we allow opportunities to slip by? How often we do not realize the good and perfect will of God, and do not reach out to touch him as He passes by. This was the beginning of astoundingly wonderful things to happen.

My husband was a different man, but I was even stranger to him than before. He often said that it would be better if I became a nun, because I had an insatiable hunger for the Word of God and wanted to read the Bible all day long.

The more I read, the more exited I became. The Word was alive for me, it had new meaning, not a story for people of bygone days, it spoke to my heart, and I discovered many precious promises. The question was this, was all the promises for "those" days, as my minister had said, or was it meant for **ME**, for **Now**. **What was of practical use NOW concerning my daily struggles here on earth?**

I asked God, how many of the promises I might appropriate for myself? He answered me with a parable. The Amplified Bible defines **a parable** thus:" **It is stories by way of illustration.** The Lord said to me: "If somebody goes to a restaurant, and orders a meal for $7.00, he can stir around the food, pick at this or that, not actually eating or enjoying any of the food. But, (the Lord said) when you go, you enjoy everything! Nonetheless, bear it in mind, **the person who was just picking at the food, and you who enjoyed all, both has to pay the same price! $7.00!All My promises are fully paid for, it depends entirely on you, how many of them you want to enjoy and use. You may enjoy and use just a few, or some more, or all of them!**

Therefore, dear reader, YOU have to choose, you may ABUSE or USE, ALL of God's promises! It's entirely up to you.

8

Every day was a new experience, (and it still is, with Jesus.) Let me tell you about one of the first things that made me realize that a BIG change had taken place in me. Do you remember, my sister used to frighten me, by just being silently behind me, this caused me to swear of fright. My kids, enjoying this tremendously, risked a hiding for the joy of seeing me frightened, plus to hear the vocal "excursions"!

I was putting away some glassware in a cupboard, when my eldest son, Rian frightened me. I very nearly dropped all the glassware, chills were running down my spine, **But not a single swearword came!** My son ran away, fearing the usual hiding. I then had a much bigger, much more awesome fright! —My legs became totally lame. I clearly realized that **God working in His mysterious way, had removed all those nasty curse words** which usually were like a string of beads, if the first came, all the others followed!

How awesome, how mighty, how wonderful and loving is our God! I hated the swearing, but could not stop it, however hard I tried. Thank You Lord, I still get frights, even though I do not want to, but every time after a fright, when no swear words come, I praise You for deliverance!

[My little three year old granddaughter, Savannah, discovered that I get a fright if she creeps up behind me. I told her not to do that. because I would go through the roof if she does that. So she implored me to go through the roof, because she wants to see me do that!.]

Peter and I were both smoking, but now had the desire to be free. I would pray for deliverance, and then smoke again, pray and smoke and smoke and pray, this happened over and over again. One day I was praying very seriously about this, telling God that I did not want to turn my face away when I had to pray for somebody, because I did not want them to smell that I smoked!

God clearly spoke to me: **"You say that I have to set you free,** but you enjoy smoking very much, **and do not really want to be free."** I was aghast! I sat upright! I thought it over! I realized that what God said was true! My deceitful hart was exposed! Oh! No! Woe to me! **I was so much ashamed!** What a terrible shock! **I lied to myself!**

I prayed, and told the Lord, that, for the first time I understood what the Scripture meant in **Jeremiah 17:9" The heart is deceitful above all things, and it is exceedingly perverse and corrupt and severely, mortally sick! Who can know it (perceive, understand, be acquainted with his own heart and mind)?"**

I totally lost belief in my own heart, I realized just how easy it is to deceive and fool, not only others but also yourself. I had to find a way, and realized this: the best way to defend is attack!

Well, having realized my weakness, I talked to our enemy, I said: "Satan, I do not like to talk with you, but I want you to come near, I have something to say to you. You certainly won, I am addicted to cigarettes, I cannot quit, I cannot set myself free, You Satan, have won! **But now, I do not come to you in my own strength, or in my own name,** or in my own power. **I now come against you** in the might, the power and the strength, of God, and most of all, **in the Name of the Lord Jesus Christ,** the Name above every name. I want to dare you to try to make me want to smoke, or to give me the desire to have a cigarette, because every time you do that, it will remind me to pray for the worst sinners I know."

So, every time when it was as though I could smell cigarette smoke, or the inside of my mouth just screamed and drooled for a draw, I would close my eyes (if I could) and pray quickly! "Lord save Jannie, save uncle Faan, and **Before I could mention the third name, the desire totally left me.** Satan realized that it was more expedient for him, to have me to quit smoking, than for me to be plucking others out of his might, and robbing him of those he was misusing! You are welcome, I have no patent rights on this way of defense, use it any time freely, this definitely always works for me.

Young people say to smoke is Cool, Oh **No! Satan makes you a FOOL.**

Later I had a problem with insomnia. I felt extremely tired all day, but sleep evaded me at night, this went on for quite some time. Then the Precious Holy Spirit reminded me of **my 'Secret' Weapon! When I could not sleep, and cannot sleep, I pray. All too soon I am very sleepy, and can enjoy rest!**

Once, I had the most weird, rude, even pornographic thoughts and pictures about others in my mind, every time I wanted to pray. Oh, I was devastated. I tried so very hard to keep my hart, this mortally sick heart, pure before the lord. I did not even had such bad, bad thoughts when I was not a child of God. Where did they come from? Why now?

The Public Prosecutor, our main enemy, **Satan,** brought condemnation upon me. "You have such a pious face, you're trying to bluff others, hey? How little do they know what goes on in your mind! You just pretend to be a Christian, but you have a filthy mind." This went on for about two weeks. I became desperate, one day I knelt and prayed, I said to the Lord, that I was ready to give up, I could not go on like that, I have never had such ugly thoughts even before I knew Him. It was totally unwanted and undesirable to me! **God clearly said to me: "This is not of yourself, the enemy gives it to you" I was stunned! What a revelation! The mean beast! He, Satan, gives me the thoughts, and then blames me for them.** I immediately knew what to do! Every time a bad thought came, I said, oh, **Satan, thank you for reminding me, it's time to pray again.** It still works perfectly, and effectively! Or I tell him it is time to praise the Lord, when something bad happens!

A young Christian once said, he had watched older Christians, (people who had walked with the lord for a longer time) and he saw that they are also prone to make mistakes. The Lord reminded him about a demonstration golf game he went to. Gary Player, a very well known

South African golf champion took part. His first hit landed the ball in a bad place, a rough place! My friend was disgusted, how could such a man play such an amateur hit? But, Gary looked, and looked again, studied the ball, the green, the surroundings, took out one club, decided against it, replaced it with another, then, patiently stood still, aimed, and hit the ball right onto the green!

The Lord told him: Though older Christians also make mistakes, even as Gary knew how to get out of the bad place, because of former experience, just so, older Christians get out of trouble easier, by confessing their sins and because they know the power of God, and know scripture promises on which to stand!

9

Well, many supernatural things happened after we became Children of God. We had a black man who was totally illiterate. He had to go for his drivers license, but, only at the thirteenth try, did he succeed, because he could not read.

Then Jack accepted the Lord as his Savior! He came to me and told me that God had told him, that he should get a Sotho Bible. This was amazing, because he belonged to the Xhosa race. I bought him the Sotho Bible, and incredible, as it may seem, he could read that fluently. Jack could read nothing but the Bible. He was thus able to read, and preach the Gospel to the other black people. If he looked at any other written words he could not even spell it!

Jack and I had a wonderful relationship after that. During prayer one day, God told me that Jack had to pray for a big black woman. She had cancer in her female parts, he would recognize her, because the lady would be wearing a black beret and a black dress, and she was very fat!. When he came to our house that same day, he told me that God had told him to go to a farm about thirty miles away, he even got the name of the farmer, which he did not know. I told him what God had told me, then, after prayer he left on his bicycle. He got there while the grown up people were still working. There were about thirty small homes, then the Lord told him to go to the last one.

As he came around the home, the big fat black lady was sitting on a chair in the doorway. He was amazed! After greeting her he asked how she was, she then told him that she was very sick, and she had tremendous pain in her lower abdomen.

He recounted to her how the Lord had sent him, and how the Lord had revealed her sickness to me. She was very touched, she asked him to pray for her. However, when he was praying, the Lord told him that she was using the dry bones that the witch doctors use. He asked her if she used that, she then asked if it was wrong. He told her that it is an abomination to God, because it is a spirit of divination. She said she did not know that it displeased God, but she promised she would never do it again. Jack prayed for her and she was instantly healed. He came back rejoicing!

I taught the ladies working for me, never ever to put paraffin into a soft drink bottle, like Coca-Cola, or any other, because children might drink from the bottle. Should they choke on the stuff, paraffin is deadly when it enters the lungs. Elisha, did not heed my warning, she put the paraffin in a coke bottle, and my baby, Karel, took hold of the bottle and drank! He choked, and spilled some paraffin on his clothes! She was very frightened, because she knew it was her fault. Being guilty, she did not call me, and my baby became unconscious. He continued to cough, and she tried to bring him round, to no avail!

Suddenly I had an urgency to find out what he was doing, I saw that he was unconscious. When I held him, I smelled the paraffin! I realized that **only god could save my child!** I took him in my arms and called on God! In such a situation, you cry out loudly, because of the urgency of the situation, there is no time to waste!

My husband wanted to call an ambulance, but we realized it would take at least an hour to get to us, when it would be too late. To drive to the hospital would also take too long! There was also another Christian, uncle Mac, he prayed with us. After a while my son regained consciousness, sat up and said he wanted something to drink, he was thirsty.

Believe me, it was not at all difficult to praise and thank God! Karel, suffered no after effects, except that the skin on his chest was burnt from the paraffin. An open reminder of the wondrous miracle God did!

The next day the lady who was responsible for the accident came to me, with her hands in her sides, she asked me in a strange hard, daring way; **"Missis, Why? Why? Why?"** I said "Why what, Elisha?" **She**

said, "Why your child not suffer, why isn't he sick today, why isn't he coughing? My child drank much less, we took him to the doctor, we did everything for him, and he nearly died! He is still not healthy even though it happened six months ago."

I said to her, "Elisha, I have been telling you about Jesus, but you did not want to believe what I told you, now You have seen with your own eyes what He can do. Don't you think you also need to become a child of Him, so that He can assist you, when you get into difficult situations?" She was very happy to accept Him then, and thereafter, she and Jack had a prayer meeting with me every morning.

I come across so many people who say to me: "Oh, we are all children of God. He created all of us, didn't He?" Well, yes, He created all, but then, I ask them the following question: "Do you take any responsibility for my children? Do you buy their clothes and food? Do you have any authority over them?" Of course the answers are all negative. So, remember there can be no authority without responsibility. Then I tell them: "Unless you accept Jesus Christ as your own Personal Saviour, you are not a child of God. Therefore, he has NO responsibility for you, and no reason to look after you, or help you!" Beloved reader, have you accepted Jesus, so that you can be sure that you have a heavenly Father, Who surely would take responsibility to look after and help you?

At a church meeting, a stranger came to us. He told us, that the Lord had revealed to him, that the Devil wanted to take Karel's life by drowning. He said that he had prayed for him, and God would spare his life. A few months passed, and we nearly forgot the warning.

We had a dam on the farm, with a pavilion next to it. It served a dual purpose, we could irrigate our garden, but it also served as a swimming pool. It was very nice to gather on the pavilion, for a barbecue and a swim. The children played there all day, in the summertime. We were not worried about Karel, even though he was the only one who could not swim. He did not want to come near the water, nobody could entice him to swim, at all.

He was playing on the pavilion, pushing a little cart, when his foot got caught in something, and he fell into the dam! There was nobody with him, but by the grace of God, His elder brother, Rian heard the splash of the water, and his scream, and came to his rescue. We then remembered the warning, and thought that it was the fulfillment of the prophetic warning! We were only to find out much later, that the evil one was not yet finished!

During that time I tried to be obedient, to do all God told me to do, without anybody to teach me. The Lord would tell me to go to the hospital. He would then reveal to me, for whom to pray. One day I went to a hospital to pray for our friend's son. He had leukemia in such a bad way, that the doctors did not expect him to live long.

After we had met Jesus, they avoided us, but when their child was dying, they remembered, contacted us, and asked me to visit their son. I went to pray for him, the result was extremely astounding, two days later he could go home. **The doctors then said they must have made a wrong diagnosis! No Ways! Jesus healed him!**

While in the hospital I saw an old man, who was unconscious. The Lord told me to anoint him with oil and pray for him. The nursing sister told me that he had been at deaths door for weeks, but could not surrender to die.

Because the Bible in **James 5:14 says: "Is any one of you sick? He should call the elders of the church to pray over him and anoint him with oil in the name of the Lord. And the prayer offered in faith will make the sick person well; the Lord will raise him up. If he has sinned, he will be forgiven."** I spoke to him, because even when someone is unconscious they can hear, although they cannot always respond. I told him, that I want to anoint him with oil, and pray for him. A deep satisfied HMMM came from him, when I said "Lord please heal this man" a very negative sound, impossible to write came from him.

I said to the old man: "If you have sinned, God will forgive you, because the Word says so." Again the HMMM, "And he can also heal you" again the negative response. I said: "But Lord, if he wants to go home, please forgive him all the sins, that the Devil is accusing him of, and take him home soon. "HMMMMM" Because I am anointing him for forgiveness. He died peacefully. Please remember that unconscious persons cannot respond, but can definitely hear. It has happened numerous times with me, afterward they would testify they knew I was there, and heard everything I said and prayed.

I was leaving town, when the Lord told me to pick up a man five miles out of town. At first I argued with myself, people do not stand five miles out of town to find a lift, it has to be my own imagination. Anyway, when I got there, sure enough, the man was there. I would not have stopped, had the Lord not given me instructions. It was an old man, with very thick spectacle lenses, it seemed to enlarge his eyes. He saw me remove my Bible, for him to sit in front. He asked me whether I was a child of the Lord, I said yes, he said he too was a child of God. I asked him where he was going.

He told me that his daughter lived in a town nearby, but that he was in no particular hurry to get there. He had been in another car before me, but when he wanted to talk about Jesus, the man told him very curtly, that he had to keep quiet, he didn't want to hear anything about religion or God. Well, he asked the driver to stop, because he did not want to waste time in his car.

That was how the Lord delivered uncle Mac five miles out of town, for me to pick up! A red letter day! He told me that he was God's roaming hiker, going to wherever, with whomsoever he got a lift. He had no claim to fame or greatness, he was very humble and without pretense, but the most amazing signs and wonders happened through him.

He was not fluent of speech, because he grew up in Lesotho, therefore Sotho was his best language, with English second and Afrikaans, our home language third. I heard that **he too had received the Holy Spirit and spoke in tongues. What a relief, I found somebody else**

who had received the gift of the Holy Spirit! It made it more real to me.

He became like one of our household, he appeared and left at any time. We accepted and loved him. He faithfully brought his small monthly pension for us to use, and that was like manna from Heaven in those difficult times. The Lord seemed to stretch the few Rands tremendously. Thank you uncle Mac! Thank You Lord for sending uncle Mac our way, our lives was tremendously enriched by him.

One Sunday he was with us, I was preparing to go to church, so, he asked me to which church I was going. Well, since I knew only the traditional church my parents attended, I told him so. **He then invited me to a Pentecostal church, but I was scared,** I had heard weird things about such churches. It was, the people told me the "sects" so, the Lord might not want me there.

I had another problem, I had enough petrol to town, and money to buy enough to come back, and get to town again. The town that he wanted me to go to, was further away, so I would not be able to get there and back, and to town again. So I had to go to **The One Who could tell me what to do.** I prayed and **told the Lord my problem,** (as though He did not know it already) I said to Him, if he wanted me to go to the other church he had to give me money, a Rand, that time about a Dollar and a half. I rested my case!

I had a bath, and when I took my underwear out of the drawer, a very, very dirty old Rand note fluttered to the ground. It was torn in half with a only a small part holding it together, in another place it was torn right through but pasted together with sticky tape. Well, I had my answer, **I had to go with him, uncomfortable as I might be.**

At the church I enjoyed the singing, even though it was totally different from what I was used to. Uncle Mac testified how I picked him up, and said I would also like to testify! Oh NO! **I was totally out of my depth,** a strange church, strange people, not used to talking to strangers, much less to testify. I told the people that the Lord had saved me, also that I love anybody who loves the Lord, and anybody who loves the Lord and wants to visit us was welcome. (Totally not what I would have liked to say, remember—I had a difficult husband at home!)

The sermon was good, and at the end of the service the pastor told everybody to wait till he could get to the door. **No escape!** I thought he would not take me up on the visiting invitation! Not so, he said that he also loved the Lord and would like to come to visit, I had to give him the directions to get to our farm. I was scared of Peter's reaction!

Two days later he and another pastor came to visit us. Thank God, they had much wisdom, and did not pressurize my husband at all. That was the beginning of a lifelong love and friendship, both pastor Melck and Peter has already passed away. That's where we found many more people filled with the Holy Spirit.

We went to a conference of this church, uncle Mac came too. After the service, a man came to us, he spoke excitedly to uncle Mac, he said he had been looking for him for a very long time. Uncle Mac could not remember him, so, the man told us the following story.

They lived on a farm, next to a river, when, one day, uncle Mac got off a car again, because the driver did not want to talk about the Lord. Another divine appointment! He walked to their home near the road, asked for something to drink, and found that they too were children of God. They were still sharing some testimonies, when the farm workers came running for help. They were extremely anxious. **They said the wagon and team of oxen got stuck, in the muddy path through the river, it had rained upstream, and a wall of water was coming,** which would sweep away the wagon, and drown the oxen.

Uncle Mac went with the brother and the workers in his truck to the river, they found that the wagon wheels were sunk into the mud, to over the axle's. **The situation was desperate.** Uncle Mac spoke to the workers in their own language, Sotho, **he told them not to shout at the oxen, not to hit them, only to wave their whip's long lash over them, he told them God wanted show them His power. He repeated that to the brother.**

The worker waved the whip over the oxen, and then to their amazement, the wagon pushed the oxen out of the mud! There were shouts of joy and fright when this incredible miracle happened. They were barely on the banks before the waters came rushing past. **The workers all accepted the Lord that day, they said: "Truly a God that can save and do what happened that day, must be worshiped"** Uncle Mac always remembered only the more "insignificant" miracles that happened, he stayed humble, because he realized that God did all, not he!

A sister in the Lord Hettie Gouws, who always gave him a meal, was very busy once, she murmured impatiently "Why does he always turn up between meals, especially when I am very busy" She decided to give him one, instead of two fried eggs. As she broke open the egg in the pan, there was a twin egg inside, she heard the Lord say: If you do not want to give my child two eggs, I will do it!"

Thank You Lord, for sending uncle Mac to us, it was a privilege to know him, he always had a joke to tell, or a wisecrack, because he was full of the joy and the compassion of the Lord.

Uncle Mac, came to us regularly, but stayed away for quite some time. Then I became very worried about his absence.

One day I prayed about him, and asked the Lord where he was, and why he did not turn up. The Lord showed me a vision. I saw Uncle Mac walking, and saw how he stepped into two loops with his feet. Then I saw how the enemy pulled his feet from under him! I was extremely, disturbed, and made inquiries to find out where he was! Eventually, I heard, from his children, that a car had bumped into him, and flung him against a wall. He had been in Hospital for a long time, and the doctors said that he would never be able to walk again. He was far away from our farm, in a Johannesburg hospital.

Peter had to go to Pretoria for his patent business, and I insisted that we go to see uncle Mac. It was, at about nine in the evening, when we got to the Hospital. Peter stayed with the kids in the car, and I went to search and pray for uncle Mac. Fortunately the nurse allowed me to go to him, when she heard that we came from far.

He was so bewildered and lonely, it took a while for him to realize that it was me. The joy, and gladness and appreciation, when he recognized me were boundless! He was totally overwhelmed! I anointed him with oil, and prayed for him. He looked much better when I left!

Three days later, his children brought him to the farm. He had discharged himself from the hospital, and insisted to come to us! **He said that God had healed him, he just had to learn to walk again!** To know **uncle Mac, was** to know **faith in action**. He struggled in the long corridor of our house, but kept confessing that he was healed by Jesus' stripes. It did not take long before it became a reality!

After we moved to town, he still visited us. We were in another part o Johannesburg, visiting with people. When we prayed together before we left, I saw uncle Mac in a vision. The Lord told me that we had to go to his children to pray for him. A little while before that, he had told us, that he was not going to shave his beard anymore, since he always cut himself while shaving. In the vision however, he did not have a beard. Peter, as always, was quick to spy on me, and asked if he had a beard or not. I dodged his question, because I thought I had made a mistake.

When we got to his children's home, he was sick in bed. He had deteriorated and was practically just a little bundle of bones. He was so extremely happy when he came out of his kind of coma, and recognized us. We prayed for him and went home. Two days later, Peter went to pray for him again. God had told Peter to go to anoint him for his departure from earth, because Satan was accusing him of things of long, long ago. He was so relieved when Peter told him that the enemy was as always, lying to him. He found peace, and passed away two days later!

See you soon, uncle Mac, then we will rejoice before the throne, dance and recount all the answers to our prayers, miracles of God's love and care!

Hettie was one of God's choice servants, she had a heart for those in need. Many a time I found the clothing and food needed for the people I was helping from Hettie. One day the Lord told me to go to a certain sister, I had to ask her what she needed the Lord to give her. She would not tell me at first, but I insisted that God told me to ask her and that she had to specify her need. She told me that she, her four children and her husband had only two sets of clothes each, so she had to wash each day. They were going to visit family, and she had asked the Lord to provide enough clothes for them not to have to wash every day while she was away. When I got home there was a message from Hettie, she had so many clothes her storeroom was overflowing, would I please come to get some! **The synergy of the Holy Spirit is Amazing**. Needless to say, all the clothes fitted, everyone in the family was fully catered for, I only had to deliver it. Thank you, Hettie!

She had used the same slimming drug Peter used. She also suffered the same after effects, and problems. She died prematurely because of that.

10

Peter was still very skeptical, and unsure, about the visions uncle Mac and I received. What happened to me on a Sunday proved the reality of such visions. Early in the morning, I was praying and worshiping, mostly in other tongues, when I saw in a vision a canal. The canal comes from an irrigation dam about 30 miles from our farm. The highway to my in-laws crosses over it. I was totally unfamiliar with the area, except for passing over the canal.

Because I was worshiping, I did not want anything to interrupt me, I kind of pushed it away from my mind. Again I saw the canal and I ignored it again. Suddenly I thought of **Sameul whom God had to call three times, and I said: "If You Lord, want to reveal something to me, I am willing to listen, and look!."** For the third time I saw the canal, as though we were in a car, driving over it. Directly after the canal, we turned right into a dirt road, and right again at the first road, crossing over the canal, then I saw a small house on the right side of the road.

Involuntarily the question arose in my mind," **Who stays there"** I **saw** the letters Marais (it is a very well known surname in South Africa.) But, why were the first part capital letters, and the second part in small letters? I queried: **"What do they need?"** I saw an old man **walking with difficulty, The Lord said to me: "He has very much pain in his legs, you have to go to pray for the healing of his legs."**

It was time to see to breakfast, and to get ready for church. I told Peter about the vision and that we had to go there after church. He called his brother who stayed with us. He was a representative and worked in that area, he asked him if he knew about the canal. He did know the canal, and about the house too, but, he said, the surname of the people staying in the house was Bezuidenhout, not Marais. My husband looked very happy to prove me wrong. I said I don't care, the MARais people must then be visiting there, **God does not have time to waste, I believe Him.**

We went to church, had lunch with our Pastor and his wife, and all the while it was raining heavily and it was very cold. Peter declared that the only good place to be, would be to rest in his own bed, he was not going anywhere else. I told him, I would then take him home 10 miles, come back and go to see the MARais. When he saw that I was determined, and was definitely going, he decided to come along. He thought it would be a good time to prove that the visions I was seeing, was pure nonsense. He said I always wanted to see and look at comics whenever I prayed. Our dear logical husbands, they always wants proof! They think, to see is to believe, while faith is, believing and then seeing! However let me continue!

We drove in pouring rain, uncle Mac was, as usual, with us. It is not very easy to do the Lords will with five busy children in a mini bus. They had agreed on only one thing, and that was to disagree! I was getting extremely uneasy, what if it proved to be a hoax as Peter said. This was absolutely strange to us! I reasoned with the Lord, I told him if He did not help me and give me courage, I might tell Peter to turn around. That would have been just what the Devil would have liked!

Peter asked me how on earth we would be able to go into the house in such pouring rain? **I said, wait till we get there, the Lord would help us. We have to obey, He will make a way!**

Unbeknown to me, God then gave Peter his first **Word of Knowledge. He knew that he Knew, beyond a shadow of doubt, as soon as we would be near the canal, the rain** that was coming down so heavily, **would STOP!** He argued and wondered how this could possibly be. Sure enough, about half a mile from the canal it seemed like a water tap or faucet was turned off! It stopped totally, and the sun came out, when we were at the canal. Yes, we found the gravel road, turned right, and right again, to cross over the canal. HEY! HEY! **There was** the house, exactly as the Lord had shown me! It was real! **Hallelujah it was real!**

Before I could say anything, Peter stopped by three young black boys, he asked them where Mr. Marais stayed? They answered that they did not now, but if we turned right to another house where a school bus was, we could ask there. I was totally dismayed to say the least, when Peter turned right to go to the other house! I said **here is the right house, why go to another?** Peter said, you saw there was no sign of life, all the windows were closed. (It was because of the rain.) OH! NO! **He was being his "old" spiteful self!**

He stopped at the gate of the wrong house, it had a dam of water under the gate. The thought of taking off my shoes and pantyhose, to walk in the muddy, dirty, icy water to open the farm-gate, gave me the shivers. I turned to uncle Mac, I asked him to pray for us. He offered a very short simple prayer: **"Lord, we came all the way to do Your will, kindly undertake for us, in Jesus' name, we thank You, Amen."**

One of the black boys knocked on the window, because he had followed us and was probably expecting some money. Excitedly he said, and pointed to the other house, **there is the house of Mister Marais! Exactly as the Lord showed me!** SPOT ON! Hallelujah!

Well, well, well, the whole day I was very small and subdued, Peter being the big and tall one. To my shame, I have to confess to you, it was a most pleasant feeling, to have it change so suddenly and to have it reversed completely, I felt ten feet tall! Peter turned the mini-bus around. When we got to the other house, a boy opened the gate for us, Peter drove through, and stopped at the kitchen door, "Well," he said, not too happy, **"You go in, it is your vision,** I do not know what to do."

I went around to the front door, unsure, how to go about it, I knocked and waited. A woman opened the door, she said "Good afternoon, I am Mrs. Maree but we say MARais. God knew of this discrepancy! He knew it was very important to them! He brought it to my attention, to be sure we were at the right place. I introduced myself, I said that I am Fine', and told her, that while I was praying that morning, God showed me their house and Surname, as MARais. Therefore, we were there and I did not know what God wanted to do. She invited me to come into their home, her father in law entered the small lounge, walking with difficulty. He introduced himself: "We are Maree but we just say MARais" Another confirmation. He went out of the room, and her husband came in, he said: "Good afternoon, I am Maree, but we just say MARais." (O, Lord, How Great Thou Art!) For God to reveal everything so clearly!

Peter came into the lounge, with the old man, who had fetched him from the car. Peter later said, that when the old man stumbled out, he knew it was the man with the sore legs! The Lord told him to let go of his lethargic ways, to get out of the car. Instead of witnessing, I had to tend to the kids. Suddenly they all had runny tummies. When one got out of the restroom, the other went in. All the while Peter talked to the people, and I had to be nursemaid! It did not seem fair! Even so, have Your own way Lord! [It was to be like that, all the time, till Peter passed away!]

They told him that they belonged to a "church" that has no real respect for the Bible. This church, believed that what the priest said, was the word of god. [Their god!] However, they were tired of the priest, he was no good. He had lied to them, and did not do what he promised, so they had stopped attending that church. Later, we prayed for the old man's legs, and for the healing of all his body. We also prayed for all of them, to be able to understand God's wonderful love. That God cared so much about them that He sent us there, from far away! We invited them to visit us, because we could see they were very unsure about us, and about the way we came to know about them.

We were puzzled, and we wanted to know why God sent us there? We learned later that a lot of their family who were in the same church, came to repentance, accepted the Lord Jesus and started testifying to them, but they would not listen or accept their testimony! The family began to fast and pray for them, so, God sent us there, in answer to their prayers. GOD ANSWERS PRAYERS!

The Marais family visited us, came to church with us, and their lives started to change. The man's legs were healed, and a new life dawned for them. I do not know what happened to them, because they moved away without leaving an address. Therefore it remains as one of the Unfinished Mysteries to be solved in the hereafter. We planted, somebody else would water, but God, gives the growth. Praise to His name!

11

Suddenly my energy levels seemed to drop drastically. I could not understand what was going on. After four children most mothers think they know all about being pregnant. Therefore, I thought I was dying slowly of an unknown decease! However, after three and a half months, when I went to the doctor, he told me that my fifth baby was on the way! Surprise, surprise, fortunately it was a very happy surprise. The doctor told me I needed to get a blood transfusion, because I did not have enough blood. He seemed surprised that the baby was still alive. I did not want a transfusion, so he gave me some capsules.

We were in church the Sunday after, but I was so weak that I told the Lord I would not be able to get up and walk out of church, He had to be quick to help me. When the service ended, I remained seated, I could not move.

A lady came running to me, she said she does not understand what was wrong with me, but God told her I was very weak, and needed strength, she had to pray for me. The Holy Spirit's anointing came over me, I felt power surging through me and I was strengthened instantly. I could walk out of church unassisted! Three days later the doctor told me, he never had anybody reacting so favorably to the capsules. I said to him, it was not the capsules, somebody had prayed for me, **God touched me, and that Prayer changes things**. He did not comment.

he rest of the pregnancy was uneventful, except that the baby developed over much! A week before the baby was due, the doctor wanted me to have cesarean, he said it would be impossible for me to give birth to such a big baby. Peter agreed with him, but I told him that I had four normal babies without knowing the Lord, and **I could not for a**

moment accept that He would leave me in the lurch. God is absolutely faithful!

Suffice it to say, it was the most astonishingly, wonderful birth, I was so extremely aware of the presence of the Lord, I sang: "Jesus break all the fetters" and felt myself relaxing, all the while, till after his birth! One of the nurses was amazed, she asked me if I was as relaxed during the birth of my other children. I told her, that it was that way because I found the Lord in the meantime!

My big son, Jakes, weighing more than nine, and a half-pounds, were born, nearly effortlessly. The doctor was flabbergasted! I sang the same tune, using different words: "Jesus heals all the wounded," and I literally felt Him healing me. Back in the ward, I was overcome with gratitude and joy, I asked the Lord to speak to me concerning the amazing birth of my son. I opened the Bible and read: Isaiah. 66:8. "Before Zion (Fine') travailed she gave birth; before her pain came upon her she was delivered of a man-child." I do not think any reply could be more clear and explicit than that! Hallelujah!

Notwithstanding my joy, I was unhappy. OH! We ladies are definitely different, sometimes difficult! Men, Please make a note of this! Write it clearly on the tables, or is it the note books of your hearts! It was my fifth child, and never with any birth, did Peter bring me flowers. His thoughts were not on my level of thinking. He, never till the day he passed away, brought me flowers! The other mothers received the most beautiful flower arrangements I had none! I surely did not want to feel unthankful or despondent, I had over much to be thankful for! However, I too would have liked some flowers! Maybe it sounds inconsequential to you, but, know this, as food is the way to a man's heart, so is flowers the way to a lady's heart. Please remember, prevention is better than cure, give the flowers while you and your wife both can enjoy it, now, not later because you are feeling guilty.

I cried, and I felt sorry for myself, I then felt cross with myself for feeling that way. A Crazy mixture! Finally, I asked the Lord His opinion about the matter! I cannot find the real scripture, since I do not have my Afrikaans Bible with me. It was, however spot-on as usual. It was about David, it said that when your thoughts multiplies, (as mine certainly did,) God would sustain you, with His love and mercy.

How wonderful to know that we ALWAYS have the privilege to enter into His presence, to know that we are ALWAYS welcome in His love!

Living on the farm, we had chickens that I raised, but once I became tired of chicken meat. I told the Lord how thankful I was, that we did not have to go hungry, like millions of others. I told Him, that I would gladly eat chicken again, if only I could have a piece of beef that day. About two hours later, a spiritual brother came to visit.

This man had been to the mental hospital quite a few times. He used to say that none of the people, who told him that he was mad, had a certificate, to prove that they were in their right minds. He had such a certificate! However, he was totally amazed and bemused! He said, he could not understand why God would send him from town, to bring a piece of beef to the farm!

I started to weep, and told him that he was absolutely in the leading of the Holy Spirit! I told him how I had asked the Lord for a piece of beef that morning! He was overjoyed, when he realized that he had not made a mistake. I can but say, that God uses even the despised, to fulfill our prayers and desires! James. 4.2 "You do not have, because you do not ask God" 2 John 3.21 "Dear friends, heats do not condemn us, we have confidence before God 22 and receive from Him anything we ask, because we obey His commands and do what pleases Him" I hope, if you had a problem to ask anything of God, that this scripture will set you free to ask, of a loving Father. He does not give grudgingly, but delights to supply our needs, and our desires. The Bible states, that God loves a cheerful giver! Would He be anything else than a cheerful giving God?

12

Brother William Burton, the first missionary to the Congo came to visit us. He asked Peter, my husband, how the crops were doing, Peter replied that our situation was very drastic, if we did not get rain within two days, our losses would be severe. He immediately lifted his hands and said: **"Father, You have never said no to me yet, send us some rain today, in Jesus' name, thank you Father."** Peter's and my reaction was to think: "Brother this is the Free State, there is not even a cloud in the sky, it will take much harder prayer than that."

That evening we had one and a half inches of rain! Our neighbor got stuck in the mud on our road, so he came for help and wanted to know if our reservoir broke, or where did the water come from? He was amazed to hear that God had sent a cloud to bring us the necessary rain. None of the other farmers had any crop, only us.

Br. Burton told us awesome testimonies about his life with Jesus. He was part of the elite in England. He would have inherited a title, but because he followed Jesus his family disowned him. He wanted to become a missionary, so, he asked various mission departments to allow him to go to the Congo, but they all declined. They said, because he had no training, he did not qualify. He felt heartbroken and rejected, he sat down in a park and said: "Lord, I'm an ass, nobody wants me, I'm an ass." The Lord spoke to him and said: "Open your Bible, I want to speak to you." He had his New Testament in his pocket, he opened it and read: **Matth.21.2 "Saying unto them, Go into the village over against you, and straightway you shall find an ass tied, and a colt with her: loose them, and bring them unto me. 3. And if any man say ought unto you, you shall say, "The Lord have need of them;** "So he rejoiced, knowing that the Lord needed him.

Eventually he and two other men sailed for Africa, however, both the other two men died of some kind of fever. He had a hard time with the bearers, they were lazy, superstitious and fearful. Eventually they were deep in the jungle, when they saw some warriors coming. They left Br. Burton and ran away. He saw a gnarled old man, his hair already gray, he was bent over, pulling himself along with a stick. Tremendous compassion and empathy filled his heart! He went up to him, laid his hands on him and asked the Lord to heal him. Instantly the old man shot up, straightened, and was healed! When the black warriors fell down and tried to worship him, he tried to make them understand that it was not he who had healed him, but God. He stayed with them, because his bearers never came back. He set about learning their language.

He used a folding knife, he kept in his pocket, to entice a young boy, to teach him their language. Br. Burton wrote down all the words, and names of everything, in a phonetic way, so, he was later able to translate the Bible into their language. When he had made some disciples, and could speak and understand their language, he decided to go to the headhunters, to bring them the Gospel. He did not want anyone else to accompany him, as he did not want to jeopardize anyone else's life.

The headhunters caught him, as he had wanted, and took him to their king. He told the King, and all else, that he came to tell them about **Jesus the Greatest King!** The king got very impatient, he said he wanted to taste a white persons flesh, he never had that before! He waved his mangled arm to indicate to the warriors to take him and cook him! But, instantaneously, his crooked arm became healed! They fell down, wanting to worship him, very scared and superstitious! He told the king that the **King, Jesus the Only Great King,** he had tried to tell him of, **healed him. Now Jesus had shown him His love, His might and His compassion by healing his arm!**

Many, many, more wonderful things Br Burton told us about the mission field. At one time he had to have all his teeth pulled. England was very far away, and there was no one to make him a set of dentures, so he prayed and asked God for a second set of teeth, which he received. **Nothing is impossible with God! IF "Only" we will believe!**

The mission station was later ransacked and burnt, also his printing machines, and he had to flee for his life. He lost his wife on the mission field! All his hard work seemed in vain and futile, but every morning he would say: "I am the happiest man alive, if there is anybody happier than I, I would like to meet him!" Because he knew, the One he had worked for, does not forget any "Work" we did for Him!

William Burton,did not die, he just left to go to heaven, without being sick! While visiting in Johannesburg, he had tea and cake, with his hostess, and enjoyed it very much. She went into the house and left him on the balcony for a few minutes. When she came back he had stepped over the line, he had departed and was gone to heaven! I do not have space enough to tell you more about this faith giant! Brother Burton, I thank you for your spiritual input in our lives, I look forward to meet you again!

We had fun too, God is not pious or religious, The Lord has a fantastic sense of humor, and if you would only look, you will find a lot of humor in the Precious Bible! I will later share with you some humor I had with the lord.

Something evil attacked Peter in his face. All over his cheeks up to his eyes and eyebrows, it started burning and itching and it was extremely painful. We had never even heard of such a thing. The doctor could not fathom what the problem was. He prescribed some cream and ointment, but the ailment grew worse. It was like a thick scab, he looked fifty years older. He could not rest, day or night. Because of the pain and irritation.

He did not want others to see him because of the way he looked. We phoned pastor Melck, and asked him to have the congregation agree in prayer for Peter. He had this tormenting demon for about three weeks. While the congregation were agreeing, God spoke to a brother, to go to pray for Peter. He had another urgent agenda of his own, but agreed to go to our farm first.

When he came, he told us that he did not come for a visit, he did not have time to spend with us, he only came to pray for Peter, because God told him to come. He anointed Peter with oil, said a very short prayer, and **God did a miracle!**

All of the insufferable pain and agony, seemed to fall out of his face! He was healed instantly! Obedience, is the center of God's will, everything seems **So easy!If we obey!**

He left about twenty minutes after he got there, and we could not stop thanking and praising God! The "thing" on his face had looked like a giant inflamed cancerous growth, but disappeared instantly after prayer!

As I am sharing with you, the Holy Spirit brings back more and more supernatural happenings in our lives. Therefore, I want all of my life to be a continual thanksgiving. I will definitely need eternity to be able to thank our Heavenly father, Jesus and the Precious holy Spirit.

13

In South Africa, we have our summer holiday or vacation, in December. So while our children were still in school, we used to go to the sea. We were staying near Port Elizabeth with friends of ours, for the vacation. It was a beautiful day, but I had no desire to go to the sea. The children and my husband kept on urging me to change my mind, they wanted to go for a swim, but I declined. At last, at about two o'clock, after a lot of pressure,I consented, on condition that we go to Van Stadens River Mouth.

It was the 24th of December, a lovely summer's day, and we had the lagoon all to ourselves to enjoy, because all other people had gone to do their last minute Christmas shopping. Because of my fair skin I have to stay away from the sun, but decided to play with the two youngest boys in the lagoon, since no other people were around. I went to the rest rooms, to put on a long sleeved top over my bathing costume, and a hat. It looked funny, but prevented me from being burnt.

When I came from the dressing rooms, I saw that Peter had walked through the wide lagoon, and he and our youngest son, Jakes were playing on the other side. I waded through the water and when I reached them I asked Peter where Karel was. He told me that Karel had gone to search for his tube, which the wind had blown away. He said he was going to look for him, because he suddenly felt uneasy, so he left Jakes with me.

I played with him in the water for about five to ten minutes, then three young children walked from the sea, into the lagoon. They could have passed on dry ground, but walked into the lagoon. When they were in the middle of the lagoon, about fifty yards from us, I heard one of them shouting: "Somebody help, there is a child here who has been drowned!"

My first thought was: "Shame, the parents of that child came for a holiday, now they will have to go back with a little corpse." Two of the children waded through the lagoon to the other side, holding the little body, the other boy ran to the camp for help. I said; 'Lord, I know nothing about resuscitation" Clearly the Lord said to me: **"But you do know how to pray!"** I said O.K. Lord, I will go to pray.

When I got to the two children and the little corpse, I looked at him, his face were terribly swollen, blue about his mouth, his eyes were closed and there was sand all over him. It was a little stranger, somebody else's child. **Then! A terribly rude awakening! A sudden and total switch!** I looked down at the swimming trunks! No longer some other person's child! **It was My Son! MY Son Was Dead!** OH horror of horrors. The realization! No one could help but the Lord! **No one could bring him back to life, only the Lord!** That's why the Lord said to me;" But you know how to pray!" **HE meant me to Pray!**

Exclaimed! "This is My Child!"

I took control over the situation! I turned him over onto his tummy, and I started pumping his lungs, as well as I could, But, **I Called on God loudly,** while doing that. I did not know how to pray, or what to pray, I only knew **Romans 8:26says: "In the same way, the Spirit helps us in our weakness. We DO NOT KNOW WHAT we ought to pray for, but the Spirit Himself intercedes for us with groans that words cannot express."** I prayed in the Spirit, **I cried** in the Spirit in tongues, **I called** and cried out in my need and agony to **the only One Who has power over life and death!** My thoughts were exclusively on Karel, **OH! God! Please Help Me! You alone can give my son back!**

I do not know how long I prayed. It was quite a while before Karel began to utter soft sounds, a while later he cried louder and louder, incoherently! I realized: **"He Was Alive! Karel Was Alive! Thank GOD! He's ALIVE!"** Reaction then set in, my knees began to tremble, and when I looked up I saw a whole case full of all kinds of stainless steel instruments for resuscitation, with a doctor standing by!

Peter had gone to look for Karel, but could not find him. Our other children, Elna, Rian and Carise saw and heard me praying and calling on God. They saw that Karel was dead, so Rian ran to fetch Peter, telling him that Karel had drowned. He came and stood by, unable to do anything, but to pray in the Spirit, until God resurrected Karel! A crowd had gathered around us, without me noticing anything! They came to watch the drama.

God had kept the doctor quiet till after He had restored my son's life! The doctor then said to me:" Lady, it seems to me you don't do this quite right, give me a chance." After a while he saw that he could do nothing more to help. **Karel was completely revived!**

The doctor then told us to wrap Karel in a blanket, to open all car windows, and drive as quickly as possible to the hospital. He said he had to warn us, that when somebody had been without oxygen as long as our child, it should invariably be expected and accepted that **there would be brain damage. Not a good message at all!**

Even to this day I am extremely sorry that we did not testify to the people looking on! We were so overcome, with thank-fullness, for the wonder God had performed, in bringing him back to life, that it did not enter our minds, to share with the onlookers what had happened!

We drove off, praising God all the while. Our children wanted to know if we were **going to the hospital, but I told them that there was no point in going there, God would not do the impossible, to give back his life and still had him to go to hospital.**

We stopped on a hill overlooking the lagoon, all of us prayed together, and we definitely had **no difficulty in thanking God.** We rebuked all bad after-effects, also his fear of water! We drove home to our friends and **there was nothing at all wrong with him!** Not physically or mentally! Hallelujah!

He was an excellent student, and he did very well at school, he got three A's in grade 12, to prove that **God does not do anything half-way!**

Let me assure you, **the switch over from "your problem," to MY problem, "your son," to My son, left an indelible impression in my mind and spirit**. Something like this does not just stick to your skin! It has helped me to be able to "walk in the other person's shoes," to be more sensitive to another person's pains, heartaches and problems. **Nothing in our lives happens just by chance. What the Devil intends for bad, God turns around for our good!He makes stepping stones out of stumbling blocks.**

Thank You Lord, that the pastor who warned us that the Devil wanted to kill Karel with water, had prayed and **canceled it, long before! God is ALWAYS faithful.**

14

My husband prayed and asked the Lord to speak to him whether we should move to Johannesburg area. (He now also asked for a scripture.) He opened the Bible at Jonah 3:1 "Then the word of the lord came to Jonah a second time.2. Go to the great city of Nineveh and proclaim to it the message I give you."

So, we had to find a place in the big city, we knew not where. Our pastor friend, his wife and children, had moved to a congregation in a part of the great city. He called us and told us of properties selling at very reasonable prizes, and that we should come to stay there and work for the Lord, with them.

The problem was, how reasonable the properties might be, we had no cash! We went to have a look at some houses. The one we decided to buy, the agent said, was the only one we could not buy on mortgage. Hey! **He did not know that nothing is impossible with God!** We did buy that house, so the 31st of July we moved in. It was bitterly cold, in the heart of our winter! It was also in the middle of our school year.

We had moved out of an extremely comfortable,modern house on the farm. It had five bedrooms, three bathrooms with three toilets, a lounge, family-room, large kitchen with separate pantry, a garden to dream of, garaging for five cars, a swimming pool and many fruit trees. The house we moved into had four bedrooms one lounge and one bathroom, the toilet was outside, quite a distance from the house. **Whoa! That was my nemesis: (according to the dictionary) an unusually tenacious opponent or antagonist, an instrument of retributive justice. (tending to reward or punish)** In my case **no** reward, just punishment!

71

Seven people with only one bathroom, seven people with urgent calls of nature. Standing in a line outside! Some really taking their time! Something had to be done! A corridor with an unnecessary door to outside the house, lent itself very well for the addition of a toilet. The problem: No Money! No Window! We got the toilet, but the rest was still absent. On a public holiday, when all shops were closed, my husband decided that the toilet, [potty in America]should be done before evening. He said to me **"You have been praying long enough**, today you have to **believe and have the window ready before lunch"**

I was desperate. **Lord Please help Now!** Eventually I thought about a friend doing alterations to houses, I called him, he said **he had just what I needed,** he had just such a window, I do not have to pay for it, I can fetch it. Hallelujah! What a relief!

The bathroom! Oh My! Daddy's hairbrush was used, there were wet towels, badly deformed toothpaste tubes, dirty clothes, wet floor and once again, some stayed in the bath too long! Oh, no! There were endless irritations. **Dear Lord, Please help!**

One day while praying about this problem, **in a vision God showed me** that our bedroom had a corner sort of cut out, and with just two walls and a window added, it would be big enough for a bathroom. Hallelujah again. We knew where now, but How to do it? We needed: Bath, basin, toilet and another window! This dear reader, is practical living, in the here and now. In Him we live and move and have our being!

Once again Peter started building the walls, with bricks the former owner had left on the property. Once again he said: "You have prayed long enough, the walls will be finished tomorrow, then I will need the window, the day after I need the bath, basin and the toilet." How Now? Having just **one recipe makes it easier, Lord Please Help Now!**

I am eternally thankful to King David who said in **Psalm. 38.22 "Come quickly to help me O Lord my savior." Psm.40. 13—O Lord come quickly to help me. Psm.70.5 Yet, I am poor and**

needy, come quickly to me O God. You are my help and deliverer; O, Lord, do not delay. Psm.141.10 "Lord, I call to You. Come quickly to me. Hear my voice when I call to You." This is the New International version, in other versions it uses the word Haste instead of quick. I do not know about you, seldom do I have a need that does not require to be helped in haste or quickly. Let me proceed!

I called my builder friend again, he said he had removed a bay window consisting of five smaller windows, I could have it for free. Exactly right again! One window fitted the bathroom, four windows were still available. Someone else needed a window, and the other three were precisely right for the garage we turned into an apartment! God sees the end from the beginning! Now for the rest of the things needed!

A friend of ours called, she needed a truck to fetch something, she asked if I could help her, I said yes. We drove to a factory, where she asked if I would pray for her while she went in, because she needed a bath, basin and toilet and wants to buy it wholesale. I exclaimed, that **it was exactly what I needed**. They owed us some money, so she said: **"If you pray,** and I can buy the things here, **I'll buy yours too."** Behold, I went home with all our bathroom necessities! Thereafter, Daddy had his hairbrush to himself, and there was so much more peace!

Mike and Santa are the people where my husband first heard the voice of the Lord. I want to share this with you. Mike brought an exceeding clever man to our house, he had three doctorate degrees, but he was an agnostic, so Mike wanted my husband who also was an agnostic before he met the Lord, to deal with him.

They started talking, the subjects became more and more surreal and difficult. A visiting Pastor talked of miracles, but this man laughed. He had lived in the East and saw operations done by hand, organs removed, cancers cut out and all kinds of sicknesses being healed by the power of the occult. No miracle like that could change him.

Eventually, they were stalemate. I sat praying for Peter for wisdom. Peter said: "In the beginning you told me that you look after about 24 stray cats. Why do you do that?" (oh! the smell in that one bedroom apartment) He said: "The cats are born because the people who should take responsibility does not do that. I am a responsible person, therefore I have to take the responsibility to look after these strays." Peter said: "Do all the cats respond equally well to your responsibility?" He said: "No, I have to admit, some respond better than the others, some stay wild, they screeches and scratches me if I want to stroke them, others love to be cuddled and stroked."

Peter asked: "Tell me, do you like all the cats equally well, or do you prefer those who respond better to your responsibility?" He said "I have to be truthful, I prefer those who like me to touch, cuddle and spoil them! They get the best food and attention. Peter said: "Well, do you see that Mike cat, this Peter cat and Fine cat? **We respond so much better to the love and responsibility of God than you! That is why** He does so much more for us, and why we **get so much more of His attention.**"

He became very quiet, his eyes grew bigger and bigger, He looked at Peter, and looked again, I could see him reasoning with himself. Eventually he said: "I MUST be Colorblind! Will you please pray for me, I want to receive God's love and responsibility too!"

Are YOU responding to God's love and responsibility, or are you screeching, scratching, and shying away? He is waiting Isaiah 30. 18 (K.J)

A friend of ours Bill, was also a kind of agnostic, maybe just indifferent to the Gospel. I felt very concerned about him, so I invited him to visit us, even though Peter said he would not be interested at all, in spiritual things. Bill said he would be with us at 6 o'clock, in time for supper.

As soon as he accepted the invitation, a foreboding settled on me, I knew that Satan would try to kill him before we could talk to him. I phoned and asked various people to pray with me, I kept praying and asking God to keep him safe, I was in turmoil the whole day long. He did not turn up at six, then seven, eight, and nine o'clock passed without him arriving, at half past nine he arrived. I was furious!

I said to him: "How could you do this to me, I was so scared that you would not get here alive, I travailed in prayer the whole day asking God to help you, and to save your life!" He looked dumbfounded, he sat down and said; "Honey, did you pray for me?" I said: "This is the understatement of the Year! I did everything, praying, crying, weeping and calling on God for you to be spared! And you had me wait and worry for such a long time!"

He said: "Maybe this explains it, come Honey, let's go out to the car, I want to show you something!" He took me outside, his car was parked close to the light. He studied the car and showed me two small dents in the body of the car, at last he took out some horsehair from between the door handle and car, then he told me the following.

Because there was no speed limit in our country at that time, he was driving at 100 miles per hour, because he was late for our appointment. A horse ran directly into the path, right in front of the car. There was NO time to swerve away, NO way at all to miss it! He collided head-on with the horse. He felt the terrible crash, he heard the crunching of metal, he heard the horse scream and neighs, saw the horse land on the car, go right over the hood and roof, waited for the window to break, waited for pain to strike him! Nothing! He thought, now I am unable to visit Peter and Fine'. He stopped, got out of the car, looked at the car in the moonlight and found no evidence of the collision, even though he stroked all over the car with his hands! He pulled off the road, turned the car in such a way that he would be able to see better in the headlights when another car came along. He waited, trembling with shock! At last a car came, he got out and looked, and looked in the lights of the other car, and found nothing wrong with the car.

Because of the accident he was prepared to listen to us, my testimony that we prayed for him shook him. Later than 12 o'clock we prayed for him, I asked the Lord not only to forgive all his sins, but also to heal him totally, if anything was wrong in his body. About two weeks later, the Lord told me to go and visit him. When I got there, he laughed, he said he expected me. He should have had a hernia operation that day but ever since I asked the Lord to heal him, he felt different, and realized that he had no trouble with the hernia that plagued him before.

While I was still there the doctor called, extremely agitated with him for not being in hospital. He told the doctor he had been prayed for, and that he got healed. The doctor screamed over the telephone, I could hear him from afar, he said flue, or a headache can go away, but not a hernia. The next day he examined our friend for a whole hour, searching for the hernia, but could not find any trace of it! All the glory and Praise to the Lord!

15

Friends of ours mentioned that they wanted to go on a tour of about eight countries, they wanted us to come along. I was terribly scared of flying, and I did not know whether God wanted us to go on the trip! I prayed fervently about the tour, until eventually I said to the Lord, He knew the Bible much better than I. If He wants me to go, He has to give me a scripture with the word "Fly." I opened the Bible and read: **Psalm 90.10 "The length of our days is seventy years – or eighty, if we have the strength; yet their span is but trouble and sorrow, for** they quickly pass, and **We Fly Away!"** That was clear as clear, no argument could annul that!

However the fear remained, and I asked the Lord to set me free from that. The morning we were to fly I said, "Lord, it is very high up in the clouds, will You help me there too? Speak to me from the Bible, Please! I read: **"Psalm 36.5 Your love, O Lord, reaches to the heavens, Your faithfulness to the skies"** I have one consistent problem! **How to thank the Lord for His Love help and faithfulness!**

As far as money exchange, it was very good, in 1972, we received $1.35 for our South African Rand. However,it became less every year, when I came in April 2002, we had to pay R11.98 for one dollar! How gruesome! Try to multiply everything you buy with 12! That is why I am so thankful for all those who have contributed to my stay in Colorado Springs! Especially my landlord and landlady, Bruce and Esther Bowman! Back to the testimony!

We visited eight countries, had many experiences of the favor of the Lord. I want to share only two with you. We were in South America in Rio De Janeiro, and our friends liked to visit old churches and structures of a by-gone age. I was tired of that, and got very excited when I found a Christian Book shop. This is what I wanted! I live in the present time!

Conversation with the sales lady was just about impossible. Eventually I closed my eyes put my hands together, pointed to heaven, and pretended to pray. She understood at last, that I meant Church, Pastor, and Assemblies of God. She said: "AH Assembleias De Deus." [I do not know the correct spelling] I realized she tried to say Assemblies of God! She told me she knew the Pastor, she would call him immediately, he is an American. When I talked to him and told him that we were from South Africa, he said we had to wait right there, they would come to fetch with a minibus, all seven of us.

When they came, the pastor told us they were having executive meetings, with pastors from all over that country attending, there were about 500 pastors together. They took us to the church where we had to wait in the meeting till lunchtime. God gave me a vision, about someone with a problem as big as the Sugar-loaf mountain. The American pastor gave Peter and me , a little time to share with the pastors. I told them about the vision, and that God said the problem would disappear. [The next day a pastor testified, that God had supernaturally taken care of his Big problem the day before!]

At the end of the meeting, all people got up to leave. Some came to greet us, but we could not talk to them, or understand what they said to us. I saw a short stocky man coming towards us, everybody tried to touch him, or talk to him, he seemed like a magnet. I asked the Lord why he was so popular, the Lord told me, that it was because he walks in The Holy Spirit. Peter, (my husband asked the same question, he later told me, the Lord had told him that the pastor was a spiritual giant)

The seven of us, and some of the Pastors, were standing together, waiting for the American pastor. Somebody spoke in tongues, there was a silence, and one of the pastors interpreted. The interpretation sounded like tongues to us too, so we asked the Lord to give us the interpretation, because we also wanted to understand what He said!

Somebody spoke in tongues again, and one of the pastors interpreted. There was a pause, then Peter brought an interpretation, and this is what the Lord said: "In vain do people try to become one, in vain do they look for unity without Me, for without My Spirit there cannot be any unity. The love you are experiencing today is because My Spirit of love is here to unite you, no matter what nationality you belong to." Again tongues and their interpretation, then Peter's: "I want you always to realize that only love can bind people of different backgrounds together, not man's love, but My divine Godly love, is the only way to unity. **So, as you are now one in My love, it is for you to enjoy the unity and My Love!"**

The spiritual giant then took the hands of one of our group. I had tried to talk to this man about the Holy Spirit on the plane, but he told me he had his church, and was not open for any other influence. Anyway, the pastor took his hands, bent his head over their hands, and he started praying and weeping. His tears were flowing unashamedly onto their joint hands. The next minute the man threw up his hands in the air, and he was baptized mightily in the Holy Spirit and spoke in tongues! WOW! The giant then went to another one of our group who was back-slidden at that time. He duplicated the procedure, and soon there was a breakthrough. With his hands in the air, he spoke in tongues and glorified God. The pastor then greeted the others just with a smile.

We shared a lovely meal, for which we were truly thankful. We did not know how to order from their menus, or what to buy in the shops. Thereafter, they took us back to our hotel, and promised to collect us the next evening for a spiritual concert. That concert was undeniably SUPERBLY done! The choir sang the musical triumph, **"A Thousand Hallelujah's,"** without a single musical instrument, only their beautiful voices were raised in adoration **to the King Of Kings !** A professor of music directed them. It was an amazing, unforgettable spiritual climax to our visit in Rio de Janeiro.

When we left Rio, we had an extra, unexpected beautiful treat, because the plane flew all along the coast to Sao Paulo. We rejoiced for the exquisite beauty of the beaches, scenery and sea. They had to pick up some passengers in Sao Paulo, one of them was a Nun.

On the flight to the USA, I noticed the Nun, because she had so much peace and serenity about her. She was not beautiful humanly speaking, but had another kind of beauty. We had to land in New York, but the plane kept circling and circling, until the captain told us that they had four and a half inches of rain in an hour. Therefore, the airport was flooded, so we had to go past to Philadelphia to land. (It was our first encounter with this city, which had a tremendous impact on our lives later.)

At Philadelphia, we were not allowed to disembark. Forty-six planes had unexpectedly landed, for which they had made no provision. We had to wait in the extremely hot plane, without air-condition, during a heat wave. It was an endeavor to save fuel. Only after an hour and half could we disembark, and by then most of the people were very agitated and loudly outspoken.

I heard that the Portuguese ladies were giving the captain a very hard time. Therefore, I followed them to the office, that was placed at the disposal of the captain. I told Peter that I was going to try to console and help some of the passengers. I did not know that he did not listen, or heard what I said.

After a while, they told us that there were buses waiting outside, to take us to a motel. I had our luggage, all our money and our passports, and could not find Peter! After a while, waiting in the line, they told us, that it was a mistake, we could not go with the buses! The buses left, and I went back to the office.

Peter and the others heard about the buses, and that they had left, so, Peter and they thought I had left with the buses! Peter became totally distraught! He promised the Lord that he would look after me very well, and all kinds of good things he would do for me! **If only he could find me again!** HA! HA!

Eventually, I started looking for the others, and found Peter in turmoil! The moment he saw me, all his resolutions left! He was furious! How could I do that to him? I asked him what he was talking about? He said how could I just disappear, without notifying him! He thought I had left with the bus, and I had all the luggage, money and passports, he thought he was totally stranded! All because my professor, Peter, was absent minded, as usual! Why do we say, deep in thought? If a car is in gear it can drive, but not out of gear! We should say we are "Out Of Thought," as my dear Peter so often were!

Everyone was tired, irritable and grumpy. In contrast, the nun, was smiling, and telling everybody that God certainly does not make mistakes! He, God, certainly have a very good reason for allowing this to happen! Inside the building, I told Peter that I wanted to meet the nun, which we did. She told us that she was on her way to Ireland, because a friend from there had written to her that she had been baptized in the Holy Spirit. Her friend had been filled with the Holy Spirit, with the speaking in other tongues. The nun told us that as she was the Mother superior of an orphanage, with hundreds of orphans to look after, she definitely needed to be endued with His power from on High.

We understood then, why God had to take such extraordinary measures to enable us to talk to her, and pray for and with her. Because we could not speak Portuguese, we did not know whether she spoke in other tongues after we prayed for her. She rejoiced that we met, by such divine appointment.

At last we flew to the Kennedy airport. We saw and enjoyed many new things, it was also the first time we had seen television! We tried to see as much TV as possible when we were in our hotel rooms. We flew all over America with our Delta pass, and we could make as many stopovers as we liked, what a BIG privilege. When we visited the incomparable beauty and awesome splendor of the Niagara Falls, we were totally dumbfounded! We could only stare in wonder at the miraculous and awesome beauty of God's creation!

Peter and I was in the very high building, overlooking the falls and the river, we were looking around on the highest floor, when I saw an artist drawing people. I said to Peter, wait a bit, I want to look how he does the drawings. I stood and watched with amazement! It was so astounding and intriguing that the artist could, with a few lines, create a likeness. I thought Peter was watching with me.

In the meantime, Peter, who had not listened, went down to the ground floor with the escalator, about ten floors down!. At the bottom, he realized with horror, that I was not with him! What to do now? He was afraid that I would come down when he went up with the other escalator. He chose a very difficult solution! He was going to try to run up the escalator that came down!

He would start running up when the escalator was empty, but half-way up, people would get on, and he would have to go down! This happened for about five times, and he was already tired! He prayed and asked the Lord to keep the elevator clear so that he could reach the top in a last scramble! I am so glad to state that God saw him in his problem, and agony, so Peter could successfully negotiate the escalator to the top. Peter's very exhausting drama with the escalator, took less than five minutes!

I was still looking peacefully at the artist, when Peter, in a huff and a puff, breathing very heavily, came to tell me, that I certainly succeeded in casing him a lot of problems. There I was, supremely innocent, watching the last few finishing touches to the drawing, how on earth could I be creating a problem for him? He then told me of his furious gallop up the escalator! Of course, I laughed, and laughed, and the more amused I became, the more agitated he became! Lots of sports, we had, because of his absentmindedness, the best is yet to come in a later Chapter!

In our hotel room, at eventide, just before sunset, I was a bit nostalgic about the kids at home, longing for them. I was also recounting how God had helped us to change our house into a home and made it livable. Peter was lying on the bed, looking at the TV, while I was washing some laundry in the bathroom, when the Lord spoke to me.

He said very clearly: **"I am going to change your living circumstances."** I said, "But! Lord, I am happy with our house, it now has two toilets and two bathrooms, and Lord, You have supplied a new carpet for our living room. We have tremendously wonderful Holy Spirit Workshops at our house each Saturday nights and," Suddenly I realized that I was busy back-chatting the Lord! I said: "Please forgive me Lord, who am I to complain when you want to change our living circumstances. You must do anything You, Lord want to do. May I tell my husband what You said?" He answered: **"You can tell him in three months time, but not now."** (Do you too find it difficult to keep a secret?)

My dear Peter was totally unprepared when I told him that the Lord had just spoken to me, very casually he asked me "Oh what did the Lord say?" I said to him "Well the Lord told me that I may not tell you now, only in three months time." This time I was totally unprepared. He jumped up, shook his finger aggressively at me, and looked furious. I thought it was totally undeserved, when he said: "I will take note of this, and if something dramatic does not happen to our family in three months time, I will tell you to your face that you are a false prophet!" I was flabbergasted! Why did it have to concern our family? It could have been one of 10,000,000 other things, but unknowingly, although he was in the wrong spirit, he was prophesying!

We decided to rent a van to drive to New York, to be able to see more of the country. It was very, very scenic, the whole way it was green and green! There were picturesque lakes, lush trees, forests, with warning signs about deer, and endless green meadows. The journey took us three days, and by the time we got to Kennedy Airport, my neck was out of joint, because I had looked around too much! I had to hold my head steady with my hands! I was in terrible pain and discomfort! We barely made it, because we forgot about the different time zones.

We were very hungry, and were glad to board, knowing that we would have food on the plane. We waited, and waited on board, for departure. After a very long waiting time, the captain told u s over the intercom, that they had received a phone call, a warning that there was a bomb on board. Everybody had to disembark, collect their own luggage, and wait until the plane and our luggage had been searched. We were still hungry, and there were no restaurants open, where we could buy something to eat. They served free alcoholic drinks to the other passengers, but we did not partake. Three hours later, we could board again, more tired and hungry! The food on the plane was somewhat stale then.

From America we toured six other countries, we saw and enjoyed a lot. We also went to Israel. Peter and I decided to go for a sightseeing drive on our own on one of their buses. We saw a big deal of Israel. At Bethlehem, we had to wait for another bus. A **Very friendly** taxi driver offered to take us for a ride uphill to see more of the town. Peter talked with him about the price, and off we went. We drove about two miles to the top of the hill, and two miles back. When I asked my professor how much he paid him, I was exasperated! He gave him about fifty dollars for that little drive!

It may seem as though we were continually hungry, if you have toured other countries, you will understand! We were again very hungry when we arrived in Haifa. I wanted to buy us a hot dog. It looked very delicious. I made the mistake of asking the lady selling the hot dogs, if it was pork. She started yelling at me in Hebrew or Arabic and then in English: "NO pork, no pork, me no sell pork! She kept on shouting it out! She was so furious that she did not want to sell me the hot dogs. There in Haifa, we realized that we would arrive in Jerusalem after six o'clock! What a shock! It was Friday, and after six in the evening, **nothing** moved! It is their Sabbath, and they observe that very strictly! Peter was very concerned, because the bus station was about six or seven miles from our hotel. I told him not to worry, I have already asked God, and He will provide a lift for us!

We arrived in Jerusalem at about six fifteen. No transport, or any buses or taxis were around. Just a few people scrambling to get home. Peter said we had better start walking to our hotel. I said no, I would rather wait for the transport I had prayed for. He started walking. Peter, was about thirty passes away, when a strange looking vehicle came along. **Oh! Yes!** The driver said. **He was going to our hotel!** I climbed onto the contraption, and asked the driver to stop next to Peter. He was truly glad to get a seat on "My" transport. I teased him all the way to the hotel, for his unbelief!

All seven of us went to the Dead Sea on one of their buses. On the bus our group sang choruses. A Jewish person, asked us what we were singing about. It is illegal to talk about Jesus in Israel, but we said we were singing about God. He then asked us about a great group of people that both he and us saw at the Wailing Wall the day before. He told us that the group had all began singing in different languages. We had also heard them, but since we do not understand the Jewish language, we did not realize that they had been singing in strange tongues.

Peter, and the three other men, of our group, floated on the Dead Sea water. Hey! The water burns like acid when it gets in your eyes, or in a sore place! It is pathetic to see the few small fishes, in the stream that flows into the Dead Sea. The moment they go out of the fresh water, they die. Nothing grows near the Dead Sea, because the water is so full of chemicals, nothing grows where that water flows. We should remember, the dead sea receives, but do not flow out. We as Christians, should share our blessings to stay fresh!

We also went to the Sea of Galilee. What a huge contrast! How beautiful it nestles between the hills. This was the first place where I felt that it was not just sales talk. The hills could not have been changed by the years gone by! Also not the stream flowing out of Galilee. **It was awesome to realize that Jesus had been on that same sea,** that Peter, and Jesus, had walked on the water there! After all the false things, like the pieces of wood that was supposedly part of the cross, and all the different graves, that they claim to be the right one. The Sea of Galilee in the open country, was literally a breath of fresh air!

My fear of flying was gone, so it never bugged me again. When we finally got home, there remained about two and a half months, before the end of the three months, the Lord told me about.

Three people from different places came to visit us, and told us that the Lord had sent them to tell us that we had to leave our congregation. We were definitely not pleased, because we had worked hard, and led a lot of people to the lord.

Every few days another agent came to us, or phoned us to ask if we wanted to sell our property. Eventually Peter said to me: **"Do you think the Lord is trying to tell us something,** or is the Devil trying to stir up something?" I could not tell him, so I said we would have to wait and see.

Once more an agent phoned and said he had a definite buyer for our property, I wanted to discourage him, but suddenly remembered what God had said about changing our living circumstances. I called Peter to talk to him, then the agent then came to see us. I kept quiet, so Peter, tired of all the false alarms about buyers, raised the price considerably, but even so, the agent left us with a written offer to purchase. The next day he called to tell us, that our property was sold!

Peter came to me after he heard that our property was sold, while I was doing our usual mountain of washing. (It was before he bought me an automatic washing machine.) The old one was called Easy, but it was definitely not easy, I had to wash and spin, rinse and spin! [Just to show you, that we too had ordinary, everyday responsibilities!]

He said we had to get a property immediately, because we need to build a house. He always was in a big hurry after he had decided on a way of action. I asked him if he still remembered what had happened at the Niagara falls. When he looked at me, in a puzzled way, I told him to think back how long ago we were there! It was precisely three months! I then told him what the Lord had said at the falls.

He quickly, instantly, immediately wanted the name of an agent in an area he liked. I said I couldn't remember, but he did not accept that, he wanted the name, now! So I said, "Lord please tell me the name, Peter is in a big hurry!" In a vision the Lord showed me a name, I told Peter, He said he had never heard of such an agent, so I said to him, there is a very easy way to find out, just look for it in the telephone directory. To cut it short, there was such an agency, and we bought the land, because it was exactly as we prayed, sloping to the north, without buildings, and a well with very soft, strong underground water. We bought it for much less than the price they originally wanted!

16

The Bible says in **Mark10.29: "I tell you the truth,"** Jesus replied, **"no one who has left home or brothers or sisters or mother or father or children or fields for Me and the Gospel, will fail to receive a hundred times as much in this present age (homes, brothers, sisters, mothers, children and fields** and with them, **Persecutions and** in the age to come **eternal life.'**

Son after we bought the new property, I went into my bathroom, and **the Lord came in behind me.** I was so acutely aware of His presence, I looked at the window, it had burglar fencing, so, I could not get out, because Jesus was in the doorway. My knees buckled and I sat down on the bath, **I said: "Obviously, Lord, You want to tell me something**, otherwise you would not be here." He said to me: **"The first of April I am coming to take your husband home."** I replied, **"Why do you tell me this so many months in advance?** It would have been easier if you had just taken him" **He said "It is because of your nature."** I said 'What has my nature to do with this?" The Lord said: **"If I do not warn you in advance, you will always blame me,** asking me, why I did not tell you, because then you could have been prepared." I said; "That is true, Lord, but it will be so extremely difficult to see him for five and a half months, and to reckon him dead, whenever I look at him! And Lord, we love each other so very much, while there are people living together who can't stand the sight of each other. But Lord, if you want to take him, then You, Lord will have to strengthen me"

How, do I ask you, can you relinquish somebody who is part of your heart, flesh of your flesh, part of your being, someone who holds your love? I was in total anguish, my mind, my body, and most of all my own spirit, was grieved in me, and I was unable to share it with anybody! I cried inwardly all the time.

I suggested that we rent a caravan to stay on the building site, to prevent people stealing our building material. It was a little naughty of me, because Peter always wanted to buy a caravan, but I am not the camping type, especially not to coop up five children in a small space, because they were suffering from perpetual motion! I wanted to kill two birds with one stone, to look after the property but also to heal him of his caravan desire. He was healed in the first few days! Thereafter he hated it, even though we had much more comforts than in a holiday camper.

Let me not drag you through all the persecutions we had, the sufferings were innumerable. Only the third building company was successful. They had to break down everything the others had done, and start anew.

I had so much stress in myself, because time was running out, and outside, because of the building problems, and with our kids in their new schools, and to keep five of them quiet when Daddy wanted to rest. Early in the morning, when they had to go to school, he needed to rest, and in the afternoon too.

Near the end of March there were just two outside rooms and a bathroom that we could occupy. I had asthma, because of the inner turmoil. I reasoned with the Lord, asked him time and again how would I, a woman be able to get all things done, in the unfinished house, without Peter to help. Elna was in hospital again, and then at this difficult time, they phoned to tell us to fetch her home.

With only two rooms, where seven people had to sleep, eat, live, cook, and do the washing and ironing! Oh, what a hard, steep time it was, to say the least. Peter was sick for the whole time and it got worse as April draw closer. Everything about the house was still unfinished!

The first day of April dawned, I waited in agony for him to depart, but nothing happened! This was a tremendous hazard! What do I do now? If I heard wrong, how would I be able in future to say the Lord told me something? I was in dire straits, in the mire it seemed. I agonized, and prayed, on the one hand I was greatly relieved that he had not died, then also I had to know what was going on!

The next day I went to dear sister Malan who had a prophetic ministry. I told her that if ever I needed a word from God, it was that day. It was imperative that I should hear from Him! We prayed, and prayed and prayed again! After a long time she said to me that she keeps on getting the same answer. She did not know if it was in connection with our building project or what, however, God told her, to tell me, there has been a change in His plans. So Be It. Lord, I thank you!

17

Mother in law! Remember **you first have a mother in law,** then **you become a mother in law!** Unfortunately, I was not my mother-in-law's choice as a wife for Peter. I hope all mothers in law or prospective one's, will take note. More than **30 years of our lives were totally wasted, because of her criticism of me. Nothing ever was to her satisfaction!**

If I put new sheets on their bed before arrival, she would lift the sheets, look into the bed and say: "Nobody can know how many dogs, cats, children or other people slept here before us!" So, If I had clean sheets ready and waiting on their bed, to make up the bed, with her, so she could see the sheets were clean, she would exclaim: "It does not even seem as though we are welcome! Nothing is ready for us!" If I served the cake upright in the plate, she would tell me that nobody can eat it that way. If however, I let it lie down on the plate, it was definitely not right either! It was agony always trying to satisfy her.

I had our five children, plus Peter, (whom she had not taught to be helpful) to look after. She only had herself and my Father in law, whom she had trained not to put a foot wrong. She expected everything to be 100% right! She had two or three servants, often I had none. My father in law, was exactly the opposite, he was the kindest man I ever came across, there was no guile in him, and he certainly was patience personified. He and my own Mother would have been two Nobel Prize winners together.

One holiday they spent three weeks with us on one of our farms, what a gruesome time. My daughter, Carise, had no real liking for my Mother in law, she would do everything contrary to what Mother wanted. There were fireworks between the two, and of course, the two younger brothers were good followers of Carise. If she said jump, they jumped, so they teased this grandmother in ways so refined that no unenlightened, would realize what was happening. But they certainly got a reaction, an explosive one, all the time. **"Your undisciplined children are without respect for grownup people!" She would say to me.** Not your children, to include my husband, it was only meant for me, just my children!

Coupled to this was Mother's dissatisfaction with me, however hard I tried to make her happy. At the end of the three weeks, we all came to our house. We urgently desired to take them with us to a church conference. They had never attended such a service, so we hoped that the Spirit of the Lord would speak to them. I was desperate. I was feeling terrible, as though I was good for nothing, I was very despondent after all the negative input from her.

I prayed that morning, and I told the Lord how totally miserable I was. I did not know if He had any use for me, or liking or hope, or if he took any pleasure in me. I did not know if I was His disciple anymore. If I wasn't His disciple, then it would not be worth living any longer! Have YOU ever been totally under the broom tree like me and the prophet Elijah, like in **1 Kings 19.3He came to a broom tree, sat down under it and prayed that he might die: "I have had enough, Lord" he said "Take my life."** I asked the Lord to speak to me in the church meeting through tongues and the interpretation of tongues, because it was of the utmost importance for me to know if I was His disciple and if he still had pleasure in me. If not? What then? However I did not wish to die!

The meeting had barely started, when a very strong anointing of the Holy Spirit came over me, I knew I had to speak in tongues, but I asked the Lord, why can't someone else speak in tongues? The Lord told me that I, myself, had to speak in tongues so that I might know, without a shadow of a doubt, that it was meant for me! I spoke in tongues, and a pastor I did not know, brought the interpretation. I will have to translate, because the interpretation was in my language, Afrikaans. This is what the Lord said.

"The road that lies ahead of you, says the Lord, is not an easy road, it is a steep, road, an uphill road. But take hold of My hand this morning says the Lord your God. Follow me, **because you are truly My disciple**. I will lead you from glory to glory and from victory to victory, says the Lord of Hosts. And see, says the Lord, My arm is a strong arm, and it is moving this morning because I see your heart, for I am the one Who tests the heart and the kidneys. I have brought you to the testing waters, and you have come into My will this morning. Therefore, listen well when My Spirit warns you, the road ahead is not an easy road at all. Look up, your help is from above says the Lord. Truly neigh you is My word, in your midst is My power, therefore be of good cheer, because **I have conquered the world**. (I spoke in tongues again)

Therefore, do not look anxiously around you, says the Lord, do not look around anxiously, because I the Lord your God is alive this morning, and I am able to carry you through all the days, even to the end of time.

Did I not choose you, **did I not call you by your name, you are mine**, and you are holy says the Lord. Holy and precious in My eyes! Therefore this morning, remember to guard My precious gifts, do not allow the enemy to break in to rob you. As from this morning, allow the fire of My power to burn brightly in your midst, and I will prove Myself as Righteous and strong and **I will lead you to victory, says the Lord!**

Nobody on earth was aware of what I asked that morning, except the Lord and me. About a year later my eldest daughter Elna got totally of track. She ended up in a mental hospital, where the doctors told us she was the worst case they ever had. She had to be in a straight jacket in total security, in a soundproof room, all by herself, because she would harm anybody who came near.

I get very, very annoyed when I hear people say: "I am mad about" then they say about what they are mad. Trivial things! If they could experience the heartache, pain, frustration, desperation and agony of a mental hospital, they would surely stop saying that. One lady told me recently, that she was mad about watermelon, a little later she was mad about coffee, then about Coke. I kept quiet, but later during our conversation she said to me: "OH, I am soooo down, I'm so despondent and depressed these days, I do not know what to do with myself!" I said to her: "It must be because you are so mad." She looked at me, she was shocked, she said: "How can you say that, what do you mean when you say I am mad?" I said: "You yourself said three times today that you are mad, did you not know that all mad people are depressed and despondent and down?" We are ensnared by the words of our mouths! Beware!

In the meantime, my heart was aching about my beautiful young girl in the mental asylum, she was only nineteen years old and she was among old ladies, old cronies. Some of them did not even seem to know they existed, they had to be fed with a funnel. Steep! Indeed Steep! **Too steep for me alone!** "**Come** to my aid **quickly, Now, Jesus!**"

Fortunately I had His hand to hold on to! I had a shelter I could run to! However, when we have to work through it, it is extremely difficult! I was busy assimilating the circumstances, trying to stay in the shelter of the Most High. But I did not desire others to see my wounds, heartache and pain, when **the Lord** spoke to me, and **said: "Go to sister Martie."** I said: "Maybe tomorrow Lord, not today, I am not fit company today, I do not want to go anywhere if I cannot encourage others." Again He said: "GO to sister Martie!" I told him again: "Some other day, please Lord Jesus!" But, then His voice came over so loud and authoritative: **"Go to sister Martie!"** I jumped up and said: "I will go Lord, but only because You tell me to go, not because I feel like going."

When I got to her house, while I was still in our car, she came out and said: "Praise the Lord my sister, **I am SO glad you came,** I am SO glad you were obedient to the voice of the Lord. **He told me yesterday** that I had to play you the tongues and interpretation I taped last year at the conference. Because I do not have a car, I told the Lord, **if He** wants me to play it for you, He had to send you here today. Please come in, I have the tape and recorder ready."

Amazed and dumb-struck at the reality and greatness of His compassion, I could not help, I started weeping. I knew in advance, with absolute surety, what she had to play for me. It was the interpretation about the difficult, steep road, but also about the strong hand that would hold me. In times of dire need and pain, when I do not know how to walk the next step, because of that interpretation I always know who holds my hand, and I know He will not let go of me! I can but say, as the chorus: "He was with me through it all." He still is! Thank You Father God!

At a very steep, steep, time in our lives, I made doubly sure that I would be holding His hand. I did a manifestation. I told the Lord, that I wanted to throw a rope right into the Holy Presence, and I want the rope to catch onto the horns of the altar. My hands might get tired and slip, but with the rope securely bound to my left hand, even if I am unable to hold on, the rope will save me, and hold me, and bind me to Him! It must not slip if I step out on it! Hallelujah! Hope is our rope!

Hebr.6.17 Accordingly, God also in His desire to show more convincingly and beyond doubt, the unchangeableness of His purpose and plan, intervened with an oath. verse 18 it is impossible for God ever to prove false or deceive us, we who have fled (to Him) for refuge might have mighty indwelling strength and strong encouragement to Grasp and Hold Fast the Hope appointed for us and set before us. 19. NOW we have this hope as a sure and steadfast anchor of the soul it cannot slip and it cannot break down under Whoever (Fine') steps out upon it (a hope) that reaches farther and enters into (the very certainty of the Presence) within the veil.

Undoubtedly, it is unnecessary for us to chew our fingernails! Unnecessary, to sigh and moan as though God has died! I detest it when I find myself moved by circumstances to be depressed or stressed!

However, then I realize afresh that the Bible says in **Hebr.12.23 You have come to God** the judge **of all** men, **to the Spirits** of righteous men made perfect."OH I do strive hard to become perfect, but! The flesh is often weak! For that we need, and have, Jesus!.

I get very, very annoyed when I hear people say: **"I am mad about"** —then they say about what they are mad. If they could experience the heartache, frustration, desperation and agony of a mental hospital, they would surely stop saying that.

One lady told me recently, that she was mad about watermelon, a little later she was mad about coffee, then about Coke. I kept quiet, but later during our conversation she said to me: "OH, I am soo down, I'm so despondent and depressed these days, I do not know what to do with myself!" I said to her: "It is because you are so mad" She looked at me, she was shocked, she said: "How can you say that, what do you mean when you say I am mad?" I said: "You yourself said three times today that you are mad, did you not know that all mad people are depressed and despondent and down?" We are ensnared by the words of our mouths! Beware!

My heart was aching about my beautiful young girl in the mental asylum, she was only nineteen years old and she was among old ladies, old cronies, some of them did not even seem to know they existed, they had to be fed with a funnel. Steep! Indeed Steep! Too steep for me! **"Come to my aid quickly, Now, Jesus!" Fortunately I had a hand to hold on to! I had a shelter I could run to!** However, when we have to work I want you to realize, though we are ordinary people, we sometimes have to bear extraordinary problems we cannot solve or humanly endure but for the Lord's help: **2 Cor.2.14 but thanks be unto God, which always causes us to Triumph IN Christ.**

He not only leads us, but our extraordinary, supernatural, amazing God helps us in and with all our human dilemmas! **He leads us to triumph!**H.

Many people prayed for Elna, some with loud voices, with shouts and all kinds of manifestations, nothing helped to calm her, nothing worked! Please get me right! I believe in all of these things, however, we learned in the "School of Hard Knocks," it is not by might, nor by (human) power, But by the Precious Spirit of God.

A pastor we did not know phoned us, he said he had heard of Elna, he wanted us to come, because he had to pray for her, because God told him so. We dared not decline the offer, however, we had reservations, because of past experiences!

We drove to the hospital, met him there, we had to ask permission to have her in our mini bus for a while, so that he could pray for her, because we did not know how hard or how serious he would pray. Most people frightened her, and we did not want to upset the hospital staff.

Oh, how wonderful! He spoke very lovingly and tenderly with her. He told her that Jesus loves her so much, and cares so much about her, that Jesus had told him to come and pray for her. There was no yelling, shouting, or big ado, he calmly said: "Father **GOD, You told me to come and pray for Elna, YOU said that YOU want to heal her, I now lay my hands on Elna, and I thank YOU for her healing, in the name of Jesus. Amen"** That was that!

The pastor left, unfortunately I do not remember his name, I have often asked God to reward him and use him. We took Elna back, and drove home with a sweet, sweet Spirit in our vehicle. Less than a week later they phoned us and asked us to fetch our Elna home, because she was healed. That was not the last time she had to go to hospital, and we always were so sorry we lost contact with that Pastor.

18

At a later stage, Elna had to go to hospital again, we had all the heartache and turmoil over again. I was a member of the local Women's Aglow Christian ladies group, they were very caring and supportive.

At a board meeting one of the English ladies, Cathy, spoke in Afrikaans, she said that the Lord had told her, while she was praying, to tell all the ladies, that each one should take a portion of my pain and worry. The Lord said I would then be able to carry the rest of the pain and worry.

Katy, an American lady, then spoke, she said she could not understand what Cathy said, but she wanted to share what the Lord had told her. How unutterably, amazingly wonderful is our Heavenly Father! She shared precisely what Cathy had shared. They prayed for me, and asked the Lord to share my burden amongst us. Oh, how priceless and precious is the flow of healing power from the prayers of concerned people. God gave me the surety that He was in control, even on the steep climb upwards.

Every time I phoned the mental Hospital, the same nurse answered the phone. If I inquired whether Elna was any better, she would say in a voice that sounded as if it came from a grave: "No, Mrs. Pienaar, she will never be able to leave here again, she will be here for the rest of her life. She is not better, she's even worse!" I told her every time. "Many people are praying for Elna, therefore I believe and know she would be well soon!" "Yes, Mrs. Pienaar that is what you say, but I know better, she will never again leave here." She would answer. Do you realize why the Lord had the other ladies share my pain and burden? Within three months she could leave, come home, wonderfully restored. Thank you Lord for your help. Let me finish Elna's story.

Because she was the eldest of my children, she used to say:" Rian and Carise are already married, my two younger brothers Karel and Jakes will also marry, but what about myself? Am I going to stay without a partner of my own, for the rest of my life?" I detest pious people, when even I sometimes act piously I hate it! Even though we try to pacify the other person, when we lack a divinely inspired answer. I always used to say that the Lord would surely provide a partner, she just had to believe in Him.

A lady invited me to minister to a group of ladies, I accepted the invitation, but could not understand why I had such a huge, overwhelming feeling of empathy for somebody who was to be at the meeting.

I shared about **11 Cor 1.3. "Praise be to the God and Father of our Lord Jesus Christ, the Father of compassion, and the God of all comfort, who comforts us in all our troubles, so that we can comfort those in any trouble with the comfort we ourselves have received from God."** I told the ladies that we do not always understand why our lives are not smooth and happy, but God uses the difficulties in our lives to teach us to identify and have empathy with others having a hard time and difficulties. I mentioned that my daughter was 31 years old, and that she was mentally handicapped, also that we have had very difficult times with her, but God had helped us, all the time.

The Lord revealed to me which lady I had such empathy for, the one I had been weeping and praying for, but she did not come out for prayer when I made an invitation after my message. I could not understand why she did not respond.

When we were having tea, she came to me, she stood with her arms in her sides and looked angrily at me and said: "Tell me how could you keep on for 31 years. I have a child like Elna, he's only 6 years old and he drives me CRAZY" I became pious again, Oh My! "The Lord gives us grace and always sustains us, He helps us to bear it patiently, we only have to rely totally on Him." We do become real Job's comforters! We make it sound easier than it is!

At home, I started reasoning with the Lord and myself. God invites us to reason: **Isaiah 1.18 'Come now, let us reason together, says the Lord."** Yes we may reason with the Lord! —We had the problem with Elna for 31 years. I was 50 years young, plus another 31 more years would make me 81 years old! Would I really have the guts and physical strength to keep on for 31 more years? A desperate tiredness settled on me, I had a total heaviness in my soul, spirit and body. What does the Lord want us to do? Most of the time God does not help us, while we are willing to endure, He patiently waits for us to become fed-up enough to want change!

We carry on, and on, and on, without taking time to consider the future. I had to decide on a plan of action. I made an appointment to see a friend, she was overseer over a lot of clinics. I invited the mother of the difficult son to come along, without telling her where we were going.

When we got there, I asked the social worker if she knew of homes where they looked after kids with mental disabilities, she did not know but promised to make inquiries, and have them send us particulars.

When we left, the other mother was extremely furious and annoyed! How dare I plan for her son to be placed in an institution! She went on and on very, very agitated. When her rage had calmed down a bit, I told her that hindsight is always the best sight. Looking back on our years of struggle, I realized that what we gained did not weigh up against what was lost with our normal children. We were unable to give the others the attention they deserved, because of our continual involved with our eldest. All four the other children were very brilliant, but it took such a big effort to keep her "intact" that our attention was not focused enough on the others. In every family the concern is always, "What about the youngest" in our case it has always been, "What about Elna?" the eldest.

The ladies' other son was also extremely brilliant, but children are very rude, and the kids at school teased him about his "mad" brother, just they like did with our children. So there is always a backlog, where one of the kids isn't normal. I told her she could have him home for weekends and holidays, if she did send him to a home, but then the constant daily irritation would be gone. It is easier to assimilate the pressure when it is not constant, day after day!

The forms from three of the homes for mentally handicapped arrived, one home was too far away, the second home did not make a good impression on me, so, only one possibility remained.

Elna loved to look at the mail, what would her reaction be when she saw the forms? What was I to tell her about this home? She would be furious! I prayed and asked God to give me the right words to answer her, I surely did not know what to say to her. She did not notice it soon, because it was in a big envelope, although it was addressed to her. After a few days, she came to me, in a terrible huff and puff and fury: "OH! You want to send me away permanently, you want to get rid of me, you and Dad want to send me to another madhouse. You are tired of me, you don't love me anymore, you don't want me with you anymore, hey!"

All the while I prayed: **"I have already asked for the right words, Lord, I need it Now!** What shall I say to her now? Lord, help, quickly!" I heard myself speaking, very calmly: "Elna, it is easy for you to say that we want to get rid of you, but other people say I am very selfish!" she said: "Ma, you are not selfish, why do they say such a nasty thing?" I was listening to my own answers, amazed about what I heard! What was going to follow? I had no clue!

"Yes, they say I am selfish, because I do not want to allow you to go to a place where other young people stay, where you might learn something new, and have the company of others your age! You do have a home, and we do not want to get rid of you, but you, Dad and me, will go there to see what it is like. If you do not like the home, well, you are not homeless, your place is with us. If we however, do not like the home, there might be someone else who needs a place like that, and we will be able to tell them about it." It was as though I was speaking in other tongues, **this was from God, not my own wisdom.**

She was quiet for a little while, turning it over in her mind, then she asked me: "How soon can we go to look at the home? I told her that we were much too busy that week, we would see at some later stage. For a few weeks I stalled her, by then the forms were lost, we searched in vain, eventually she said: "I looks as though you really are selfish, there never seems to be time to take me to the home! It is because we waited so long that the forms disappeared!"

One Friday morning, while praying, the Lord spoke to me and told me to contact the home for Elna. I said: "But Lord, You know how we have searched in vain for that forms, we cannot find it, we need it to make an appointment, but cannot remember the name. But, if You, Lord, want me to do something about it today, **help me to find the forms.**" I cannot explain these things. In the very same desk we had searched and searched in vain dozens of times, openly, **lying on top was the envelope!** The angels must have been, hiding the form!

I phoned the home, but the secretary told me that the person responsible for interviews was on leave, she would be back on Monday. However we needed to make an appointment before we could visit. So, I made the appointment for Monday. Elna was sooo exited, she could barely wait, she asked me hundreds of questions to which I did not know the answer. On Monday she dressed with care, she wore a lovely pink dress, I did her hair in a becoming style and off we went. The center is located about 100 kilometers from our home. She talked incessantly all the way, because of her insecurity, anxiety and excitement.

At the center we met the lady responsible for accepting or turning away the prospective inmates. We testified to her about the Lord, and what He had done for us, soon she was crying. She told us that she became a child of God when she was sixteen years old, but her husband was totally indifferent to the things of the Lord. **She had asked the Lord two days ago, to send people to her, to encourage her, and talk of the Lord. See! God's timing is always perfect!**

The lady asked us if we had already filled in the application forms, I told her that we did not consider that, before we saw the center, because we were not looking for a place to get rid of Elna. She said, in that case we had preference over more than 300 other applicants, because most other parents want a place to dump their "problem." She stated emphatically, Elna had to come as soon as possible.

The principal came into her office, he is a very nice person, she told him that Elna could play the piano and accordion, so his dream of an orchestra could become a reality. He got very excited, he said she definitely had to come to stay there, they need her for their orchestra! He told us that the matron would be back the following day, to give the final answer, but he said we had to be ready to have her in the center not later than Wednesday! Peter and I said wait, this is developing too rapidly, we can't keep up! God works in mysterious ways, and sometimes very quickly, to answer our prayers.

When we left, I asked Elna if she would like to stay at the home, she said definitely! I asked her if she saw a likely companion there, she said: "Yes! Very definitely, the one with the naughty face is mine, I want him!" I was amazed that she had made up her mind so quickly, and could decide so quickly.

What we did not know is that one of the female"patients' who lived there, eloped on Friday, therefore they had to fill the opening as soon as possible. On Tuesday the matron phoned to tell us that Elna had to be in the center no later than the next day, Wednesday! Everything had to be packed and ready very speedily. We took her there on Wednesday, she did not even cry when we left, because she was too exited about her new life! That same evening Hannes came to visit, he brought her two chocolates and asked her to be his girlfriend. So, it was love at first sight for both of them!

After three years of going steady with Hannes, the principal decided to do an experiment, he gave 5 couples the privilege to marry. Elna was overjoyed, God answered her prayers for a husband. He provided a fairy tale wedding dress, the bridegroom and best man's suites, all without any cost. About 250 guests attended the wedding, and I had to prepare all the food.

At Carise's wedding a few years previously, Elna made me promise that I would prepare exactly the same food for her, on her wedding day, if ever she got married, and she definitely kept me true to my promise! They now have been married for nearly fourteen years, God surely gave her the best partner in the world. Hannes is the most patient person I have ever met, they are just as much, if not more in love now. Praise our Amazing, Providing God! Praise Him for His amazing Grace! Praise the Omnipotent One! He gave her a husband!

19

At long last, the house was finished and we could move in, how marvelous it was to have space, and a place for everything, after the cramped living in the two rooms.

We did not have a telephone, because it was a new area, and there were no telephone cables. Therefore, not every week, maybe just once a month, people would pitch up for the Holy Spirit workshop. They still came, even though this house was about 20 miles from our previous one. We had glorious times in the presence of the Lord.

A brother in the Lord, Pietie and his wife Daphne, sometimes came. His work entailed doing very unpleasant assignments since he was the coroner. He had to examine people, who sometimes had been dead for a long time, or had been murdered. Death seemed to seep into his spirit, it seemed to cling to him, because he was busy with it all the time.

The first time we met them, the Lord revealed to me that a valve on the left side of his chest did not close off perfectly. We prayed for him to be healed. His wife got very excited! She said the specialists had wired him for a pacemaker, for his heart, but then decided against it. A week after we prayed for him, he had to go for his yearly medical checkup.

The doctors had him do push-ups, climb stairs up and down, walk on a treadmill and other tiresome things. Eventually he was very tired, and could not understand what was going on. He went home, but the next day they called him to come back. They put him through the same paces, until he was very exhausted. He then asked them why they were having him do all these exercises. They told him since he had a heart attack, it invariably leaves a scar, they had always found the scar during his former checkups, **but now the scar had disappeared,** so, they were searching for it, but could not find it! How great is God!

One evening they were at the meeting, and he seemed to be even more quiet and detached than usual. So I asked brother Verwey to pray with me, that God would set his spirit free. After that, Peter said that somebody had seen a vision, and had a revelation of a cross, he asked the person to please share with us. After a pause Pietie told us, in his quiet way, that God had told him, that he, being a coroner, ought to know that if a person dies, and the body stiffens in a certain position it cannot be changed.

He said, Jesus died with His hands open, because the nails were driven into his hands, therefore His hands can never be closed! We say someone has an open hand for the poor, but, **Jesus always has an open hand for all**, He is forever giving. He gives us His love, His compassion, His riches of Glory and healing, and help for every conceivable and inconceivable need a human being might have. (Oh, how I love Him, how I adore Him! Jesus, My provider1)

Then the Lord showed me a vision, I saw a centrifuge with test tubes in it, I realized that it could only concern Pietie. I asked the Lord to show it to me very clearly, so that I could be absolutely sure of what I saw, because he is a scientist, and needs absolute proof, two times two has to make four! I saw that the blood in the test tube at the right side were much darker than the blood in any of the others.

The Lord said: "He had allowed the person whose blood was so much darker, and which he, Pietie would have to test, to become sick. So that he, Pietie could reach him, and minister to him, because God had His hand on him for a specific ministry and calling. He wanted to heal him, even though he had a medically incurable disease.

Furthermore, God told me, Pietie would know without a shadow of a doubt that it was the blood of the right person. He had to look at the blood in the tube on the right hand side in the centrifuge, (my learned friend Bruce Bowman told me the name) **it would be much darker than the blood in other tubes**. It seemed a bit intricate, but I told him exactly what the Lord had said. His wife exclaimed that he only works with the blood of dead people, but he told us that he also have to make tests of the blood of living people, should the doctors require it.

I always wonder why I have such an acute inquisitive desire for all there is to know about the things of God, however I am not at all sorry about that. I was counting the hours to Monday evening, knowing that it was improbable to hear something before then. Pietie phoned me on Monday night. Even he sounded exited, he said **the blood in the test tube on the right hand side was black** in comparison to the others. The doctors had requested some tests, but he did more than they asked for, because God told us that he had an incurable disease. H e found that **the man did have a medically incurable disease** of the pancreas, just as the Lord had said. In South Africa it is called **pancreatitus**.

I then spoke to his wife, and we had a wonderful time of praise and worship over the phone. While we were praising the Lord, He showed me a vision of a man with a back-to front-collar. I did not know what it was about, so I told Daphne to tell Pietie not to worry if there was a priest present with the sick man. He had to share with him the full counsel of the Lord, and pray for his healing. We also decided that I would visit her at their home on Wednesday morning.

Wednesday at their home I found only Pietie, she had gone to buy milk He came for tea, and to meet me in her absence. I asked him if he had already seen the man, but he said he was too busy, although the sick man was in the hospital directly behind his laboratory. I admonished him, I told him the man might be discharged at any time, and how would he then be able to pray for him? It was essential to pray for, and minister to him! Since God had a calling for him, he had to go as soon as possible!

He decided to go to see the black man in the hospital, during his lunch break. The matron seemed very dubious, because it was not visiting time, however she relented and took him to the ward. There were quite a number of beds in the ward, but she took him to a bed, where he saw a patient busy reading his Tswana Bible. When the patient became aware of them, he lowered the Bible, then Pietie could not help smiling, because **the patient was wearing** striped hospital pajamas, but under the pajamas he wore **his back-to-front clerical collar!** (I told You, God has a very great, special sense of humor! He also is aware of every detail of our lives!)

After they greeted each other, Pietie asked the patient if he knew God. In a very serious, austere, prim and proper voice he said: "Well, I'm a minister of religion." He told Pietie that he lived in Botswana and came to visit in Soweto, but he got so sick that they had to send him to hospital, with an ambulance. **All other hospitals were full, the only** one where they had a **bed available, was right next to Pietie's laboratory!** (For God's appointment with him.)

Pietie told him why he came to visit him, because he wanted to tell him the good news. **He had to accept the Lord Jesus as his personal Savior, then he could be sure of his eternal destination.** He also wanted to pray for him to be healed, since God said that he wanted to heal him, Pietie also prayed that he would be successful in the calling God had for him.

The minister said: **"This is all so new to me, I don't think I have the faith to believe all this."** Pietie told him that the Bible talks of the prayer of faith, and that he, Pietie had the faith that God would do what He promised. When he eventually laid his hands on the sick man, he reacted as though an electrical shock had gone throughout his body. **Two hours later** Pietie phoned the hospital to ask to visit him again after hours, **but he had already been discharged.** God reached him in the nick of time. Inquisitive me, I wonder what the outcome of this "Unfinished symphony" would be, I would like to hear what happened to him,. because we never saw him again!

20

Because God had healed Pietie completely, he was able to find a less depressing job, with the company of the Oppenheimers, who recycled some of the gold mine dumps. In former times, the mining companies could not extract all the gold from underground, so it has become a payable concern to recycle.

Peter got involved in building houses, although I did not want him to. I wanted us to preach the gospel, and I did not trust the partner he wanted to involve. Anyhow, Pietie and family had to move closer to his new job, so they needed to find a home. A home that we built, was nearly completed and would serve their purpose, so Peter gave the builder instructions to finish the house, quickly. The day before they were due to arrive, Peter and I went to make sure that all were as it should be.

What a terrific shock, it was still in a shambles! The electricity was not connected, the house was not cleaned, the garage was unfinished and a heap of building sand, lying in front of the garage doors, made it inaccessible. We got hold of the builder, he promised to make haste, and be sure, to have the house all ready the next day.

Unfortunately, the next day only the sand had been removed and the house was cleaned, the garage was not finished, and Peter had to "borrow" electricity from the people next door with an extension cable. This was the way the Lord was using to open Peter's eyes, to reveal to him why I was uneasy about the builder.

For three months, after they moved in, every morning a pool of water was on the floor, in front of the zinc, to the chagrin of Daphne, the very precise wife of Pietie. She called twice a week to complain about the water, twice a week the builder promised Peter to see to it, all to no avail. After the third month, Daphne and Peter was at the end of their patience. Peter promised the builder, should he not rectify the problem before Wednesday, he would have to suffer very serious consequences, of which he had no understanding, again he made promises! Promises, promises!

In the meantime, I was pleading with God to help me, because Peter did not want to believe that the builder was embezzling our funds, or that he was very dishonest!

On Friday, Daphne called again. The builder had not made his appearance yet, she was fed-up with having to dry up the water every morning! It was not funny after all! Peter decided to act!

The builder was staying in a home on ground belonging jointly to Peter and him, that he had built with our money. Money that should have been used to build houses we could sell. Peter called a rich man and asked him if he was interested to buy the property, they decided to meet on the property. I went along, I wanted to go to pray with a sister in the Lord, sister Verwey. After Peter was gone, we prayed and I asked the Lord to send the builder home, and very speedily. For any reason, even for a runny tummy!

Peter was still showing the prospective buyer the house, when the builder pitched up. He was amazed, he wanted to know what was going on, what were they doing in his home? Peter told him that he was selling the house. He also told him it was because he had not kept his promises. For three months, he had promised to see to Daphne's scullery, and did not do it. So, not only was he selling the house, they were not going to build together anymore. Their joint business operations were over! It was a shock to the builder!

To conclude, God heeded my prayers, He saw my agony, and HE came to my rescue! Can you believe it, **that Friday morning was the Last time the angels poured the water out** in Daphne's kitchen! Never again did she have to dry the floor! God alone could unfix that "fix". God had succeeded to open Peter's eyes.

A month after we stopped the building business with him, we got phone calls from various companies, asking us to pay for materials delivered to places we did not build, it helped Peter to realize more how dishonest the builder was! Peter later gave him far more than we owed him, because God told him to show mercy!

Pietie started his work at the recycling mine, and came to visit us the next day, because he had a problem! The scientists at the mine were totally baffled, the security was stricter than before, the tonnage they processed was exactly the same, but they recycled a million Rands worth of gold per month less than before. Nobody could solve the problem or find the gold, so Pietie was assigned this to do this formidable task!

I said, well, Daniel in the Bible knew Who could solve problems, and I know Him too, **lets go to the Throne of Grace, to find help.** We prayed and soon I saw a ground dam with water, slake was drifting on surface of the water. It became clear to me to ask him if the water they used were the same. I had the clear impression, that, **if they used water with slake, the chemical reaction might not be the same** as with clean water. I asked him if he knew whether they used the same water. He did not know, but promised he would find out. He asked me if I knew that the mixture of ground and water they made to extract the gold, was called "slake" I did not know that!

That surprised as well as him! During inquiries at the mine authority, the next day, he found that the water they used came from underground. They told him, that because of the terrible drought and water shortage, in an endeavor to save water, **they started using the underground water!**

The problem solver, **Our Lord revealed and solved the problem so easily!** A few tests to adjust the chemical balance and the R1,000000 worth of gold were retrieved! Just my problem remains, I have no solution for that! **How on earth can I possibly thank and praise Him enough** for all the answered prayers?

When Pietie and Daphne came to bring us the good news, that the problem was solved, we rejoiced and praised the Lord for His goodness, His mercy His ability to help us in all of our troubles. While we were praising, the Lord told me that **another million Rands worth was lost every single month**. I told Pietie that, and saw him looking at me in a speculating way. I could follow his reasoning" What the Lord had done and revealed in the past, was miraculous, however, the owners of the mine had the BEST scientists, the BEST chemical analysts working for them, **it did not seem possible that they could overlook** something of such great value!

The Lord and I take such great pleasure when we can confound the wise! His tests proved that there were a million Rands worth of phosphor per month, in the same gold bearing slake! Up to that time, South Africa had to import phosphor, thereafter we could actually export! It is so exiting to be in His Majesty, King Jesus' service!

My spiritual family always laughs at me, when I tell them that when the mouse and the elephant walked over the bridge, the mouse hooked his fingers into his braces, and said: **"We surely cause the bridge to Shake, don't We?"** Just want to remind you that I, the mouse was also there when Jesus was shaking the bridge! HA HA!

21

The testimonies I am sharing with you are not in chronological sequence, I am just sharing as the Spirit leads me. It does not in the least cause them to lose uniqueness, or the revelation of the power, and love of God.

My Father in law had passed away, and my mother in law was staying in a retirement hotel, about 30 miles from our home. We had to pass the post office on our way to her, so we stopped to get our post. As I was taking the post out of the post box, a plane passed overhead, making a lot of noise, as it was going down to land at Johannesburg Airport. Involuntarily I looked up, and as I looked up the Lord spoke to me, He said: **"Shortly you will be going to America."** I said: Lord, may I tell my husband?" He answered: '**At the right and proper time but not now.**"

When I got into the car, I said to Peter: "The Lord has just spoken to me." He said, kind of casually: "And what did the Lord say to you?" A Bomb! "The Lord said I cannot tell you now, only at the right and proper time!" He exclaimed: "What's the use of you telling me that the Lord spoke to you, if you do not want to tell me what He said?" I said: "There is a very good reason for it, later I will revert back to this place and time, then you will know that God spoke to me here." He thought about it a bit and said: "Yes OK, that makes sense, I will have to be satisfied with that."

About three weeks later, we were driving in another part of the city, a plane came in to land from that other direction, and as I looked up, the Lord said to me: **"In October you will be going to America."** I asked the Lord again, if I might tell Peter what He said, the Lord gave the same reply. I said to Peter: "Do you remember the day at the post boxes when I told you that the Lord spoke to me? He said he did remember, so I told him that the Lord had just repeated what He had said, but I still could not tell him.

About three weeks later, we were having one of our Holy Spirit Workshops, when the sweet presence of the Lord manifested in a supreme manner. There were not so many people present, but each experienced Love in a different manner. Some were standing, some praying, others reading their Bibles, some kneeling, everyone was busy with the Lord in his or her own way. I was sitting on the couch, so aware of His anointing and love. Then God spoke to me, He said: **"Hold out your hands together."** (as though to receive something) I saw that **a pearl the size of a tennis ball, was placed into my hands. I said: "And this pearl, Lord?"** He said; "This pearl will be sufficient to pay for all your costs." I asked: "What costs, Lord?" He answered: **"The 28th of October you are leaving for America."** It gave me a jolt!

I went to the calendar to see on which day the 28th was, I saw that it was on a Saturday. I had not the vaguest idea on which day(s) there were flights. I went back to the lounge, and prayed, I said to the Lord America is a very big country, if He did not give me special places to visit, how would we know where to go? Then the Lord told me Kansas City and Vancouver.

Brother Kobus and his wife Norma, was also there, after tea, when they were leaving, I told them that the Lord had given me "marching" orders, and I wanted to ask for prayer, instead I heard myself say: "You must find out if you are also included!" They were living in faith, not earning a salary, so I thought, that it did not make sense! They promised to come around on Tuesday morning, for us to pray together.

Peter had a very bad cold, that evening, and I was glad I did not have to tell him then. The next day I looked for the World Atlas from Readers Digest. I could not find it, and asked Peter if he knew where it was, fortunately he knew, but he wanted to know what I wanted the Atlas for. I told him that the Lord gave me the names of places I needed to pray for. (Which was true)

There were only about three weeks left before the 28th, so I realized that we had not much time, we had to book our seats rather soon. I had previously told the Lord that I was always trying to give Johannesburg water with a teaspoon, now He was sending me to America with a teaspoon full of water, such a big country, with so many Evangelistic outreaches. It did not make sense to me.

On Monday morning, I decided to go to book our seats, however before I did that, I went to see sister Wittstock. We talked about the things of the Lord, and I told her I came to her, because I needed prayer. If the Lord showed her something, fine, if not, she then just have to pray for us, and ask for strength to do what God wants us to do. After tea and testimonies, we started to pray, worship and praise the Lord.

We had barely started praying, when she said: "Oh, I see a wonderful vision! The Lord shows me that He is giving you a very big jar, about a meter high, this jar is full of water. The Lord says, you must first take the jar, pour the water over yourself, then you must hold it up, and He will fill it again. He says this jar is so big, that you will have more than enough water for everybody wherever He sends you Wow! **That was spot-on!**"

Uncle Mac sang a little chorus, "What more, What more could Jesus do?" I also wanted to say, What more, What more could Jesus say?

Gone was the teaspoon! Hallelujah! I loved to exchange it for the big jar! She prayed for strength for Peter and me, to do the will of God, she also asked for His protection over us, and **for Him to give His Angels charge over us!**

Oh, the wonderful, supernatural ways God deals with us. He knows everything! At the travel agency I heard that there was only one flight per week to America, sure enough, only on Saturday evenings!

I got back home at about eleven o'clock, after I had booked tickets for the two of us. Shortly thereafter, Peter came back from a business appointment. I asked him if he still remembered the two times when I had mentioned to him that the Lord spoke to me. He did remember it, and I told him that I could tell him what it was about. He said very casually, that since he was in a hurry, I must tell him quickly. I said to him: "Oh, no I cannot tell you quickly, I want to give you tea, and I'll give you nice cake too!" I wanted to soften the shock a bit.

When we had our tea and cake, he asked, "What did you want to tell me?" I said: **"The Lord said we are leaving for America on the 28th of October!"**r Amer Peter jumped up and exclaimed: "The Lord cannot say that, **He knows it's impossible,** it is totally out of the question! We cannot leave the building now!" I said to him: "It is not my fervent desire to go to America, you are the head of our family, all you have to do is to pick up the phone, cancel the plane tickets, and tell the Lord that it is impossible to go! "He grumbled and said that it is not so easy to do as that! I should know that.

That night, he rolled from one side to the other, blew his nose often, went to the bathroom, and was very restless. Eventually I asked him what the problem was, was it a money problem, he said no, much worse, I asked him if he was worried about his health, **NO Much worse.** Exasperated, I said, now what on earth could be so bad? He said: **"Just think about it, I will have to preach in English!"** I burst out laughing, I was amazed that he was afraid to preach in English! You see, scripture cannot just be translated, then the gist of what is said is lost. Fortunately for me I came into contact with many English speaking persons, mostly ladies, and I read just about exclusively different English Bible translations, like New International version, King James, and The Amplified Bible. Also English Christian literature.

Tuesday morning, Kobus and Norma pitched up. And to our amazement we learned that the Lord had given them instructions to go to America. They had been telling the Lord that time was running out, it would soon be winter,[we are unable to endure the American winter,] our winters are much more mild. They were also praying for funds to go. Peter donated half of their plane tickets, so **we booked two more tickets for the 28th of October.** They had another contact in the USA. **They wanted us to go to Philadelphia,** to see Christians they knew.

The morning of the 28th, a brother came to say goodbye to them. Br. Kunz had a unique prophetic ministry, as he got into his car, he saw a vision. He told Kobus that he clearly saw the name Philadelphia, and he also saw a big, big spider's web. He told Kobus to be very, very careful, not to get entangled in the spider's web, only to help those who were caught in the web to become free.

When we came to Philadelphia, we got there, just in time to go to a meeting. Peter did not feel well, but Kobus, Norma and I went. There were quite a lot of people waiting to meet us. I knew nobody, and did not know how they believed, worshiped or what denomination they belonged to. I was therefore not biased at all. During the meeting, the Lord showed me a vision.

In the vision, I saw a very big building, it had seven pillars under the building. The building should have been sustained on and by the pillars. However, one pillar was cracked and loose at the top, not in contact with the building any more. Two others were also cracked at the top, but still in a bit of contact, even in the cracked state. At the end of the meeting I shared with the gathered people what the Lord showed me. I saw people looking at each other strangely, but did not understand why.

We found that it was a very big church, they had seven pastors. The presiding pastor had erred, and was already ostracized from the church.

The church was part of the discipleship movement, which ravished the States at that time. The members were in bondage, and we ministered to people, day after day, to set them free. We experienced wonderful revelations, and other gifts of the Holy Spirit. However, God gave us a free will, to choose. All of His gifts, are free, but we need to appropriate it, to work for us. We also experienced the love and hospitality of the people, and that love is still enriching my life now.

The people who heeded the Lord's warning, had good lives after that, even though they had a hard time to become totally free. Unfortunately, the spirit of lust, which was **transferred by the laying on of hands,** by persons who had erred, broke up many homes. It is tragic to hear how many couples divorced as a result of that. It was indeed a very big spider's web, with a lot of bondage! Because of the timely warning, **we got involved, but not at all entangled!**

Even as we have to be very careful, and we have to make sure, that the food we eat is clean and healthy to our bodies,**we need to be much more careful about our spiritual intake. It really is a matter of life or death!**

22

One of the dear people in Philadelphia asked us to go to her brother and sister in law in Los Angeles. On our way to Los Angeles, we had to stop over in Phoenix, to change planes. We had to wait for a few hours, for a connecting flight. On a map of the States, we saw that the Grand Canyon was not too far away. Since we had three days to spare, to get to California, we decided to see if we could change our plans. At inquiries, we heard that there was only one last plane going to Flagstaff in twenty minutes. So, our schedule was changed instantly. We did not then know that **we had a divine appointment in Flagstaff!**

When we arrived in Flagstaff, we went by bus to The White Angel Lodge, located on the brink of the canyon. In the foyer a colossal log was burning in the fireplace, with lots of people coming back from their sightseeing or ski tours, and others like us arriving! I turned around and saw a very big board, the notice written on the board did not spell good news!(Fortunately the Bible says we do not have to fear bad tidings) It read: "An expected twelve inches of snow by tomorrow morning, with zero visibility, maybe to be snowed in for weeks."

I spoke in Afrikaans, (our language) I said: "Dear Lord, we came here **to see the glory of Your creation,** we do not have the funds to be snowed in, and we have an important appointment in Los Angeles. So, Father, **in the Name Of Jesus, I am sending all this snow into the desert,** and I thank You Lord for a very clear and beautiful day, tomorrow, to see and enjoy Your handiwork"

Peter came to me, he asked me if I had seen the notice, I said, yes, no problem, I have already sent the snow into the desert. He got cross with me. He told me I could not just move snow according to MY wishes. Then Kobus came, read the notice, and prayed exactly the same prayer, turned around and said to Peter: **"So that has been taken care**

of. Let us make arrangements to fly through the canyon with the helicopter." I rejoiced and told him that we were in agreement, because I had sent the snow into the desert too!

After supper we prayed together in our bedroom, we asked God if here were something He would like us to do in Flagstaff. Kobus saw a vision, of a short stocky man, standing in front of his own home, wearing a clerical collar, (back to front) and he was wearing glasses. He said, the Lord told him we had to get in touch with this person! What would you do in a situation like this?

While we were in the foyer, I saw a list of the churches in Flagstaff and the telephone numbers to reach them. I told Peter and Kobus that, so they went to the foyer to write down the numbers. When they came back, Kobus started phoning, he asked either the pastor or his wife if the description did fit. The third or fourth person was the Baptist minister's wife. She said no, it does not fit her husband at all, but there is only one person in all of Flagstaff who could fit that description, that is Father C the Roman Catholic priest. Fortunately, she had his number, as it was not on the list.

Kobus phoned Father C, He described him according to the vision he saw, and asked him if he fitted that description? Father C, very amazed, said: **"Yes, that's me, but where did you get my description?"** Kobus then told him that we are from South Africa and that the Lord had showed him how he looked, in a vision, while we were praying. He invited Father C to have lunch or supper with us the next day when we were back from the helicopter trip through the Grand Canyon.

Father C then exclaimed: **"Haven't you seen the weather report? An expected twelve inches of snow, with absolutely no visibility!** We might be snowed in for weeks!

Kobus answered him and told him that we had sent the snow into the desert, and that we would have a gorgeous day. We were going to fly through the canyon with the helicopter, and would be back at about

12 o'clock. We would call him after twelve to see if he would be available to see us.

Father C said: "Unfortunately tomorrow is the only day in the year that it will be totally impossible to meet with you. Tomorrow is my birthday, and I belong to my assembly. They invite me for breakfast, for eleven o'clock tea, for lunch and dinner. I will not be able to see you."

Kobus answered him, that we still would phone him after 12 o'clock to find out if we could not perhaps see him sometime the next day, because God told us to contact him.

We went to sleep, looking forward to the tour of the next day. We were also curious to know what the outcome of the father C episode would be.

What do you think was the first thing I did when I woke up? **Of course, I ran to the window, opened the curtains! T**o see a beautiful, crystal clear sunny day! Do you understand why I like to brag about JESUS? All day and every day!

We literally had a breathtaking trip through the canyon, it was REAL cold in the helicopter, for the people from sunny South Africa! AH! The wonder of it all! To know that MY Savior created it! If there are things so beautiful here on earth, **how will Heaven be?** Far more fabulous than we can fathom! I have seen a vision of heaven, and I know! Best of all, Jesus will be there!

Back at the hotel, Kobus phoned Father C. He was astounded, flabbergasted! He said: "My whole assembly has totally forgotten my birthday, nobody has invited me for anything. **Imagine! The Lord sending you from South Africa on my birthday to invite me,** I'd be delighted to accept your invitation for supper!" They made arrangements to meet in the foyer of our lodge.

Peter had a word of knowledge, he knew how Father C. looked, exactly like a brother Gouws, we knew very well. He told me about the revelation, so, when we came into the foyer, I looked around and saw the double of the man we knew. He had a cap drawn over his ears, and a scarf wrapped around his neck, nothing of the back to front collar could be seen to give him away. I walked up to him and said: "Good evening Father C." He was astonished, he could not believe his ears, he exclaimed, pointing to his breast: **"How did you know it was me?"** Peter told him that **the Lord had revealed it to us, therefore it was extremely easy to recognize him.**

There was the very same notice on the board: An expected 12 inches of snow, zero visibility, and we might be snowed in for weeks. Kobus and I used the same recipe as the previous evening. After all, Paul said in the Bible. "The weapons of our warfare are not carnal, but mighty for the pulling down of strongholds." This snow business, looked to me like a strong hold, the enemy wanted to hold us with, to withhold us from going where the Lord wanted us to be, and doing what he wanted us to do!

We enjoyed a nice thick buffalo steak, the best we ever had! After dinner we went to our room to share with Father C. The Lord gave Peter a fantastic parable.

Peter asked our visitor if the story about the man and woman who could not have children, but caught a baboon, shaved his hair off, and tried to teach him to be their son, is also known in America? He laughed and said yes, there is such a story here, except they call it a monkey. Then Peter used his best American accent, (the man who was afraid to preach in English) and **he told us this God given parable.**

A man and a woman, decided to catch a monkey, shave off his hair, clothe him and put shoes on his feet. They gave the monkey 10 commandments to keep, otherwise he would receive correction. 1. He must not eat scorpions or worms. 2. He must not climb trees. 3. He must brush his teeth. Five rules said he must do this or that, five rules about what he must NOT do. **Oh those commands.** Oh! The poor little monkey, he had such a hard time. He got beaten many times a day, because **he could not keep the ten commands!** He became very sad and downcast, he was totally discouraged, and did not know how to change himself, to be as they expected him to be.

One evening in desperation, he said: "If there is a **God, please won't You help me, I cannot keep the 10 commandments**. It is not possible for me to keep them, I always do the wrong things, that I don't want to do. I continually disappoint my new Father and Mother, and **I am so tired of the painful discipline** because of all my wrong doings. I really tried, but cannot change myself! Please help me!"

Peter said: "Suddenly there appeared a wonderful soft glow in his bedroom. A lovely reassuring voice spoke to the monkey and said: **"You do not have to keep the commands,** and **you do not have to change yourself, little one! My Son Jesus Christ** died for you on the cross, **He paid the full, the total price, for all your wrong deeds**. He alone can change you, not to want, not to desire to do wrong. Believe in Him, He will help you." He was feeling so peaceful, so relieved, that he fell asleep, with a lovely monkey-grin on his face.

Father C Was enthralled! Peter asked him: "Father C **What do you think was the first thing he did when he woke up the next morning?"** Father C Creased his forehead and nose, he was thinking deeply: "No," he said "No, I do not know, **please tell me, please tell me, what did he do?"** Peter said: **"He went to look in the mirror, to see if he was changed.** Now, Father C **you tell me, what did he see?'** Again he concentrated intently, then he shook his head and said: "Please, tell me, tell me, what did he see, what did he see?" Peter said:

"Well, Father C h **e saw exactly the same monkey of the day before." The old man looked very disappointed,** but then Peter said: **"But, Father C—**, when he went outside, he looked at the tree which he had climbed the day before, and he had no desire to climb it. Then he saw a big stone, and because he was accustomed to do it, he rolled it over, and there was a nice scorpion! **But our little monkey had lost all desire for scorpions!** There was **a NEW Spirit in him**, not that of a monkey, but **that of a human being!**

He could now learn to talk, to walk upright, to wear shoes, to brush his teeth, and to abide in the commands of his Father. The ten commandments no longer was a burden to him, it came naturally! He eventually could learn to drive a car, and people came from far and near to look at the great wonder that had happened. **A monkey became a human being!** Then Father C. he felt the urge and desire to take the wonderful message, to his family in the mountains where he came from.

He took his motorcar and drove to the mountains, he tried to talk to the other monkeys, but they would not listen, they were absolutely unbelieving. Later, they slowly began to accept him, he told them that he could speak the language of men. They were very skeptical they said, OK, let's hear it. He read them a beautiful piece of poetry, but **they said: "It is Gibberish!" Exactly what people say about the strange tongues!**

Peter then began to liken it to an unsaved person, unable to keep the Ten Commandments, because the human spirit rebels against the things of God. When a person gets saved, by accepting Jesus as Savior, the Spirit of God changes the person, and takes away the desire for sinful wrong things. When the Spirit of God through the gifts of the Holy Spirit gives us a new language, and we speak in other tongues, unsaved people often say it is "Gibberish"

Then Kobus interrupted Peter in Afrikaans, he said: "Brother Peter, God has shown me what to do for our friend, I believe **your ministry is done, give me a chance now, I can see he's getting tired."**

Kobus said: "Father C God has shown me in a vision, that your life is like an island in the sea, very dry and barren, totally removed from the mainland, which means the wonderful gifts and riches of God. However, while I looked, I saw that God built a bridge from your barren island to the mainland. If you are willing, **I will lead you over the bridge,** as a manifestation of leading you **to the gifts and riches of His Glory."** Father C exclaimed, and jumped up! **"Lead me, please lead me!"** he said, Kobus took his hand, and lead him a few steps, then he stopped and said: "Father C, God told me, **if you are willing, I will remove your coat,** as a manifestation of **removing your cloak as a Roman Catholic Priest."**

Urgently he cried: "Remove it, remove it please." Kobus then took off his coat, and said: **"Now, remember, I am putting on your cloak again, but you will NEVER EVER again be a priest of the Roman Catholic Church! You will be a priest of Jesus Christ, IN the Roman Catholic Church!**

The presence of the Holy Spirit was extremely intense. The old man wept, he said: "I have worked for God in India, for more than twenty years, **when I came back I heard of the outpouring of God's Spirit. I heard that people spoke in strange tongues.** I heard of Father McNutt whom the Lord uses mightily for healing, and other great deeds of the Lord. **I then said, "God, I do not understand, but, God, if this is for real, I want YOU to send people to me supernaturally to tell me of the things of the Holy Spirit. Imagine, God sending you to me, from South Africa, on my birthday, to tell me this is for real! He is so Mighty! He is so wonderful!"** [What a birthday present!

We all laughed and wept together, we were so touched by the realization of the Grace mercy and loving-kindness of GOD, we were SO impressed with His love that could put all this together. **We could say with David: What is man that You should think of him!** He had compassion on Father C, maybe, He was instrumental in allowing all to forget his birthday, to give him a much better one!

He was like a man under the influence of alcohol when he left, he was filled with the joy of the Lord.

This is another unfinished symphony, I might only hear the follow-up in the New Jerusalem! The apostle Paul said, one have planted, another have watered, but God alone can give the growth.

23

Oh!, Yes!, We did fly out of Flagstaff, by the mercy of the Lord! Our plane was the last to leave from there, for about ten days, all were snowed in.

My Goodness!! We arrived in Los Angeles on the eve of Thanksgiving! Because we from South Africa, we were totally unenlightened, and knew nothing about Thanksgiving! It was a total madhouse. Traffic, and traffic jams like you have never seen, nor we! We phoned the people we were going to, but they informed us that it would take them one and a half, to two hours to get to the airport. They suggested that we should take a bus to Van Nuys, where they would fetch us, as soon as we phoned them to announce our arrival there. So be it!

At last we found a bus, went to the upper-deck and were very happy to sit, and to be out of the throng. From our elevated position, we saw a man go totally mad! He accelerated his car, drove forward, and ran over a number of people, drove backwards, and ran over more people. Later that night we saw on television that three people were killed and about five seriously wounded. Not too uneventful!

We did not know the people we were going to, we knew that he was a professor, a relative of someone we met in Philadelphia. Graciously they were willing to have us, but there was uncertainty on both sides. However, **a stranger, is just a friend you do not know!**

The next morning, all four South Africans were very eager to testify to our hosts. I could see that it was more than strange to them, this strangers with strange testimonies, from a strange country! **We were still on a spiritual "HIGH" after Father C,** so I believe we were definitely more than a bit overpowering. Our hostess, were preparing delicious food for Thanksgiving lunch!. AHH, the turkey smelled really mouthwatering! We had blueberry or boysenberry pie, and all kinds of berries and cherries, unknown in our country, what a treat. Later in the day we had pumpkin pie! My! My! What a treat.

After a lot of testimonies, our host said that the stories sounded good. But, he had heard a lot of different things that proved to be false in the end, he wanted to make an agreement with us.

He said his wife was very sick, and the doctors did not seem to be able to help her, **IF the Lord revealed her problem** to us, **and He healed her, he would** be willing to **accept what we told him, about the gifts of the Holy Spirit.**

That was a real challenge for us, but only a small one to Jesus. We talked amongst each other in Afrikaans, and we asked the Lord to manifest Himself, and reveal her problem. **So often we are too tense to hear His voice!** He has to wait for us, to become quiet to be able to hear His still, small voice in our spirits!

At last the superb turkey, and the other delicious food was ready! We sat down to the delicious lunch, talked, testified and enjoyed the meal and the company. When we were just about finished, nicely relaxed and filled, the Lord spoke to me. He said: **"She is suffering from a massive hormonal imbalance."** Sometimes it is too high, then again too low. The doctors can't regulate it. "I told Peter, Kobus and Norma what the Lord told me, in our own language, Afrikaans, and told our host that we were able to pray for his wife, because the Lord had revealed the cause of her problem. **Whenever the Lord reveals, He definitely heals!** Blessed **Jesus, He is always ready and willing to heal, in every way!**

When we told them that we knew the problem, I saw that he and his wife shared inquiring glances. We anointed her with oil, then I asked the Lord to heal her completely, I rebuked the massive hormone imbalance, and asked the Lord to restore her hormone balance totally, the way He meant it to be! When I mentioned that, **I felt her involuntary start, and he pulled in his breath sharply!**

After prayer they shared with us. Her hormone imbalance, had upset their lives, and what an unpleasant existence she had! Whenever this imbalance happened, nobody could even walk in the home, without intensifying her suffering! The hormone balance was not at all constant, sometimes it was too high, often too low, a lot of doctors and specialists had tried, but could not rectify the problem. Life was extremely difficult and unpleasant I think you guessed the rest, the Lord touched her and made a very big difference, He specializes in making a difference!

A few years later, the Professor, came to South Africa to teach the Methodists about the Baptism of the Holy Spirit! I would like to find out more of what the Lord has done in the years since we met them! As far as I am concerned, the symphony is not finished yet!

The stumbling block, the imbalance, proved to be a Stepping Stone to know and experience more of His Gifts.

24

A special friend of mine, Laverne, called, she told me about a friend of her, who had an eighteen months old boy, that had been sick and has cried continuously since birth. She asked me to go to pray for this little chap. My Mother in law, was visiting with us, and she got very unhappy if I left her to go out. As I was starting to tell my friend that I could not go, the Lord showed me in a vision what the boy's problem was. I knew then I had to go! I waited for my Mom to have her afternoon nap, to slip away.

The mother of the boy, Annatjie, had an exhibition of her lovely paintings in our town. When I got there, she was busy with some prospective buyers. The little boy sat on the carpet, making dejected, cheerless, discontented noises. I went to the child, and started playing with him. Soon he was laughing aloud! The mother rushed up to me! She Demanded to know what I had that she did not have? She said in all of his eighteen months, he had not laughed for anyone or any thing at all! I felt uncomfortable and I did not really know how to answer her. Because she was busy with her clients, I suggested she should bring her son for prayer to my home, after her exhibition,. She agreed, to come at half past four.

To pacify my Mom, I went to buy her a dress. As I was looking at various dresses, a sudden pain Gripped me in my stomach! This was not merely a pain, it was the "Pain" of all pains." I could barely breathe and could scarcely drive home! I endured excruciating pain that whole afternoon! I could not act normally, I had to lie down. It was a long wait, because the boy and his mother turned up at nearly five thirty. When they rang the bell, the Lord spoke to me! He said:

"Does it amaze you that the little one has cried continuously? What you felt this afternoon is how he felt all of his miserable,

measly, painful little existence!" The Lord had shown me earlier, that **he had a severe narrowing in his esophagus, just before it entered his stomach.** He could only eat or drink a little, till his esophagus was filled. The result was, he was always hungry, because just drops passed through into his stomach. However, he was full at the same time, if he bent over, he would spill out what was in his esophagus, whatever it was that he was eating or drinking. Furthermore, **there was a narrowing in his colon** where it joined his stomach, so his digested food passed through into that with great difficulty and pain. **He also had, the Lord said, a massively enlarged spleen! OH! MY! What a diagnosis!**

I invited them to come in, we went to the lounge, and I said that I first wanted to pray for Isaac, Icsy, as they then called him. **I had a selfish reason for the instant prayer! I wanted the pain in my stomach to be over!** I laid my hands on him, prayed, and **I asked the Lord to remove all obstacles in his intestines.** I commanded all narrowing to disappear and be healed totally, his Mother agreed, then I asked: **"Lord, Please touch his spleen, and make it absolutely normal."** As I said spleen, I heard his mom's quick intake of breath, and I knew that **God was completely right, as usual!** She did not know about the other problems, since I had not revealed anything to her.

When I finished praying, she said: "Its amazing that you should mention his spleen, for the specialists told me it is massively enlarged"

Shortly thereafter, my daughter Elna, brought us mugs with coffee and cookies. The little boy, took hold of his Mom's mug, and started eating one cookie after the other, after dipping them in the coffee! His mother could not talk to me, she watched, spellbound. Eventually, he even finished the remaining coffee! Then she exclaimed!: ."I can't believe this, he has not had one whole cookie in all of his life, now he has eaten about five or more, and drank all the coffee." He was laughing and smiling all the way, so happy to be without pain and hunger! God did an instantaneous, miraculous, total healing! Isaac, is now more than twenty years old and has never been sick again! I am absolutely, totally incapable of expressing my joy and thanksgiving for His awesome wonders!

Remember why the book is called "Stepping Stones, With Jesus" ? In my life, I had many, many stumbling blocks, so I continually need Jesus to change stumbling blocks into stepping stones. He, Jesus helped Isaac to change his, from sickness to health. "Precious Jesus, thank You!"

My friend Laverne's son was driving late at night, he was very tired, and must have fallen asleep, then he had a very bad accident. The truck he was driving left the road, and landed off the road, amongst trees, and was not visible from the road. It was in the middle of winter, **freezing cold, and far from a farm or town. He was very badly hurt, and unconscious. His chances of rescue, was according to Our minds, just about nil!** But God saw him!! **Ezekiel 16.6 "Then I passed by and saw you kicking about in your blood, and as you lay there in your blood I said to you: 'LIVE' !"**

Two gentlemen were driving home, from the same direction he came. Suddenly, the call or demand of "nature" had them stop, at precisely the spot where he had left the road! (That's what our human minds would say!) I know it was the call of God, because, his Mother, though she could not understand, had to keep interceding for him that previous day!

They got out of the truck, and were astonished, to see in the moonlight, that there was an overturned truck lying next to the road. They went to inspect, and found him, seriously wounded, and already very cold!

They covered him, and used their cell phone, to call medical response, and the police! The police, traced his family, according to the truck's registration number, and alerted them. An ambulance came, and took him to hospital. He was in a critical condition! His Mother, when she heard about the accident, called some of her prayer partners, and we alerted others, to form a prayer chain! We interceded for him, and after days, the doctors, who had No hope for him, said there was a change, for the better!

He was really critically ill, for quite some time, before he was strong enough to get out of the emergency ward. His Mom kept us informed, day by day, of the ups and downs, until we knew that he was finally off the critical list! **He has made a fantastic recovery**, totally the opposite of the prognosis of the doctors and specialists!

How thankful we are, that: "It so happened" that **the men stopped precisely there, by Divine appointment!** We do not have the ability, to thank and praise God enough, because **the Lord is Always there for us!** I praise HIM, because He gives His angels charge, to keep us on all our ways, even on lonely country ways.

Laverne's other son, bought a farm, and regularly paid the mortgage installments. Unfortunately, the attorney, to whom he paid the mortgage installments, embezzled the money, and drew up a false document. He also falsified her son's signature, indicating that the "price" of the farm was much more than it really was.

A lawsuit, concerning the money that was "lost," and the false contract followed. It was a very, very difficult and involved case. It dragged along, for five whole years. We stayed in the word, and said that **God would not allow a lot of lies to triumph!** He had a word of Prophesy, that God would help him to win the case. **The Lord also promised him, to prove openly, to the community, that the attorney was guilty, and not her son.**

It would be impossible, to relate all the drama, stress, and costs that were involved! Suffice it to say, that her son was brought to the brink of bankruptcy. Had he lost the case, he would have lost millions. However, Our Lord, made Scripture come true for him: **2 Cor. 2.14 "But thanks be to God, who always leads us in triumphal procession in Christ"**

The Prophesy was fulfilled, and he won the case! The guilty, crooked attorney, who caused all the problems, was responsible for all the legal costs of her son! We can but **Glorify the Lord!**

NB NB _____PLEASE INSERT FOLLOWING IN FORMER Testimony just after small Print NBNB.

We can say to Satan like in **Gen. 50.20. "You intended to harm me, but God intended it for good, to accomplish what is now being done, t**he saving of many lives." So this meeting and healing was by divine appointment. We invited Annatjie and her family, to visit us, I promised to look after their children, that they could fast and pray, because God wanted to give them a ministry.

When we prayed together, God told me to ask them what they desired. She said that she was painting, but, she wanted to improve her painting technique, and she wanted to be able to paint faces. She needed to find a market for her paintings too. They needed the money to subsidize their income, Annatjie said, they had already asked God for another house, since theirs was too small. While we prayed the Lord showed me in a vision, that they liked flat- roofed houses. Though I had never seen their home.

They had four children, she's an artist and her husband a professor. So I asked the Lord for a house with at least four bedrooms, a studio for her, and an office for her husband. With four children they needed a family room, too. I asked them what else they would like. She said, her husband grew up near open country, so, they would like a piece of nature next to their home! Quite a tall order, and that on a not too big salary!

I told them to start at the beginning. Firstly, to put their house on the market. Secondly, to contact the mortgage places, to find out if they had repossessed houses. We then left for the USA, for about a month.

As soon as we were back, Isaac senior called. Their house had been sold, and they had just six weeks, to find another house to buy, and to move in. They could not find a suitable home. I asked him if he did what I had told him to do? He did not remember to call the mortgage places, to hear about repossessions, but promised to do that immediately.

In the meantime, Annatjie went out with a lot of Real estate agents, to look at different houses. They were driving one day, and the agent, quite a bit irritated, asked her what kind of a home they actually would like. At that precise moment they were passing a beautiful home on a hillside, so, Annatjie exclaimed, that it was exactly the kind of home they would like! The agent jeered and said: **"It is so typical of our female specie, we want and like what we cannot afford, and what we can afford, we do not like!"**

She did not know the love and power of God working on behalf of those who love Him! **"It so Happened"** that **only one** mortgage place that **had a repossessed house,** they had **only That specific house** that **Annatjie had pointed out** to the agent! **(Is that coincidence? Not if you are a child of God!)** Eventually, they bought that house for less than half the evaluation price! Hallelujah!

The house had everything we asked for in prayer, and even more. The piece of country, turned out to be a whole hill at their back door! There were a lot of trees, shrubs, wild flowers, birds, and wildlife. They had their own private park! Plus a swimming pool! Once again, how on earth can we thank and praise Him enough!

25

Dear Christian, are you free, or are you simulating or pretending to be free? What is binding you, keeping you earthbound, withholding perfect freedom? Is it an unforgiving attitude? Maybe some sin that you kind of cherish? Uncertainty that God really loves YOU? Maybe, guilt and condemnation from Satan? Whatever it may be, the bonds have been broken already, **in the Name of Jesus! Hebr.12.1 let us strip off and throw aside every encumbrance, unnecessary weight and that sin which so readily (deftly and cleverly) clings to and entangles us"**

Sometimes we are like the donkey that was led in a circle, to grind the mill. Later, he went round and round automatically! Or, maybe like Samson? You are already free, Christ paid the full ransom, be free! Step out stop grinding at Satan's mill!

Free? Yes, we do not have to live a totally drab, predictable life! We may have exploits with the Precious Holy Spirit. If we are willing to sacrifice our comfort zone, otherwise we miss out on very exiting experiences with the Lord. In Los Angeles, we visited Universal studios. It was very interesting to see all the various tricks they have, while filming the movies. The burning house seems so real, so also the collapsible bridge, Jaws, the shark, and then we saw how they simulate an eagle flying in the air.

They have a huge cylinder that blows out a very strong stream of air. A little falcon, its foot fastened with rope, simulates flying, when it comes into the stream of air. The picture is taken from the ground, usually on a cloudy day, since it makes it look more real. This is then enlarged, blown up, to look like a giant eagle, soaring high up in the air, with the clouds as background. You must wonder what that has to do with me?

From Los Angeles we went to Colorado Springs. We fell in love with the lovely city. The majestic mountains seems to guard over the city, the changing colors of the mountain intrigued us. Every few minutes it seemed totally different. Pikes Peak, with its crown of snow, loomed high above other mountains.

The Garden of the Gods, I choose to call it God's Garden, with the red rocks and peaks, indescribably unique and awesome. We could but gaze in awe and amazement at His Wondrous Creation!

We had some urgent business to attend to, that involved someone from South Africa, but expected it to be over very soon. However, the Lord had other plans, He ALWAYS sees the end from the beginning! Soon it was Saturday, and I was thinking about going to church on Sunday. I did not want to waste my time in a Church where the Holy Spirit had no place. So, I went to the reception, and asked the lady for a telephone directory.

To my utmost amazement there were between two and three hundred churches listed. I asked the Lord to reveal to me, where He would have us go. From all the listings, I chose three Churches, and asked the lady how to find them. She was astonished, she asked me how I came to choose those three? I told her I asked the Lord to help me choose. She said, none of the three were more than two or two and a half miles from the motel!

Peter and I, differed very much in our sleeping habits. My energy level after ten o'clock at night dwindles quickly, while he liked to be awake to read till the wee hours. I love to greet the daybreak, and that was his best time to sleep. Of course, it created problems if I wanted to be up early, especially in a motel room. So, I was elated to find an Assemblies of God Church, high up on a hill, in Colorado Springs, that had a prayer meeting around six o'clock in the morning.

The first morning, being a total stranger, the Lord spoke to me. He referred back to the little falcon at Universal Studios. He told me that 99% of **His children resemble that falcon.** They **simulate freedom,** but some kind of sin or problem binds them, and hinders them from being absolutely free. He said, if I wanted to be free, I had to fly that morning! I had a lot of excuses, but he said it was my choice, to be free or stay bound! I definitely desired, and still want to be free. I went to the foyer of the church, it stretched along the whole width of the church.

People coming in, looked at me in amazement, and must have found it very strange. I would run, and then simulate flying! I "flew" for about ten minutes, then went inside to pray.

Sunday morning I got up and dressed early, took the car and went to look for the churches. The first one I did not like, the second church looked quite nice, but I had no time to find the third, I had to fix breakfast before going to church.

At the church, the usher told us, we came to the right church, they had a visiting Pastor with a fantastic prophetic ministry. That made my heart jump for joy! During the service the pastor gave his testimony. He was born blind, and at some time in his life, he said to his mother that the Lord had appeared to him during the night. The Lord told him to tell his mother to get him a white suit and white shoes, because on Sunday, in church, God would restore his sight. His mother was surprised, what does a blind child know about a white suit and shoes?

Just as he told his Mom, the Lord restored his sight, but he still has a very obvious squint, he says it is to continually remind him what the Lord did for him. His ministry was to say the least, very unorthodox! He was so full of the joy of the Lord, he danced, and rolled head over heels down the passage. He prophesied to some of the congregation, and by the way they reacted, I realized that it was true. He made an invitation, but Peter told me to SIT!!!!!! Suddenly the pastor stopped, stood still and said: "I have never had this in my ministry, but God says that there is a very strong anointing here, anyone who wants to renew their youth should come out." Guess who jumped up and said: "Come!"

Peter took my hand and pulled me with him. As soon as we stood in front, the pastor looked at us and started prophesying to us. He started with: "Servants of the Lord" He then prophesied, and duplicated a prophesy we received about a year before. He never mentioned the renewal of our youth again, but I believe the Lord did do it, for I accepted that and am still in running order! God had to use a carrot, a lure, to get the donkey, Peter to go out!

We expected to be finish the business by Monday, so when on Sunday the evening weather news said: "Heavy snow tonight" I asked the Lord to postpone it, because we did not know how to drive in snow. Sure enough, no snow that night, but the business was not concluded that day. The same weather report that night, they also said they did not know what happened to the snow the night before. I asked for another postponement, Tuesday arrived, lovely and clear. Business still not done, same thing. Tuesday evening, was a repetition. Well, Wednesday evening, I said to he lord, the business is still not done yet, if maybe He wants us to see the snow, let it be!

Thursday morning! Oh! What glory! The exquisite beauty of a glorious Thanksgiving Day, clad like a bride in the purest white! Do you realize, fear of the unknown causes us to lose out, so much, so often!

We were invited to lunch with some precious Christians, so, we drove there, very careful, because of the massive amounts of snow. The rocks and mountains were clad in their bridal gowns! Our hosts lived in a home near the golf course, close to God's Garden. When we arrived there, the golf course was covered with pure white virgin snow. I was ecstatic! We had never seen such a beautiful landscape, as far as we could see, it was stretching up and down in this superb white garment! Beautiful? Marvelous? Exquisite? Wonderful? Awesome? Undeniably a work of art! Superbly done by our **Lord Jesus the Great Creator**. No human words can describe the joy I had seeing it.

We enjoyed a very lovely lunch, the company was even nicer. If the people involved should read this, know that I have not forgotten your hospitality, and I believe God still takes care of you, even though we lost contact. I would love to renew our friendship!

At home there never is a time when all the work is done, especially for a mother. Therefore, I decided to spend a day at our friends home, who had a separate home, for people visiting them. I needed to spend time alone, out of reach of others, with the Lord. I planned to remain there from eight in the morning till three in the afternoon.

WRONG TAB It was wonderful, I could pray and praise in tongues or in Afrikaans [my language] or in English! I read the Bible, and studied related Scripture verses. I interceded, worshiped, sang ,rejoiced, and meditated on the Word! What a glorious time I had! **At about twelve o'clock the Lord spoke to me: "At twelve thirty, I want you to go home, I want you to go and make a long skirt for sister Verwey."** I was extremely disappointed!I said to the Lord: **"BUT Lord, You know that I wanted to spend time with You until three o'clock! I had planned and looked forward to this day with You alone!"** The Lord repeated his message! Hey! **Why do I always seem to REASON!** It is solely because **we do not understand God's Reason!** I said: **"Sorry Lord, I do not have to understand, if You want me to do that, it's fine, I'll go!"** He had shown me which material to use too!

Long ankle length skirts were very much in fashion. I laid the material out on the floor, and started to cut the skirt. We are about the same length and built, therefore I needed no extra measurements.

Awhile I was cutting, a neighbor came , she told us that Peter's bookkeeper called, he had to see Peter very urgently, it had to be that very same day! I could not help smiling! The bookkeeper lived about one mile from the sister whose skirt I was cutting! God knew that the delivery was organized for the afternoon! I made haste with the skirt, and when Peter wanted to leave at 3.30, I was just about finished, and could do the hand stitching in the car.

At the Verwey's home, I laughed and threw her the long skirt and said: "There's your long skirt, stop screaming in my ears!" She started praising the Lord in her own soft spoken way! Then she said: "This very morning,I stood in front of my kitchen sink and said to the Lord: "Lord, You know that sister Marie had promised me a long skirt. However for some reason I do not understand, she seems to be cross with me. So it seems I will not get my long skirt. And Lord, You know that I get pain in my legs because of the cold. Won't You **please lay it on somebody else's heart to make me a long skirt?**" She turned to me and said, **it was just after twelve o'clock that I spoke to the Lord!** She asked me to go with her to her bedroom, because she wanted to thank the Lord, and praise Him, because of His faithfulness!

Well, we had a long session of praise and thanksgiving, and we were still in her bedroom, when her husband came back from work. He usually reminds me of a very big, bright sunflower. However, when a sunflower's head is drooping it is much more noticeable, than when it happens to any other kind of flower! He was, and looked totally dejected and depressed.

He told us that his knee, which he had injured at work was extremely painful, it was swollen to such an extent that his trouser leg was tight around it. I decided to lift his spirit, by telling them a lot of wonderful testimonies, but instead of lifting his spirit it seemed to make him more and more depressed.

When Peter stopped at their gate the Lord spoke to him. The Lord told him, that He was giving him the interpretation of a vision and tongues, **he thought brother Verwey still had to see the vision.** He knew that he would totally misinterpret the vision. When he came in we moved to the lounge to pray. Instead of being glad about that as usual, Br. Verwey was not happy at all. So, Peter and I moved toward him, at the same time. I started rebuking the spirit of depression, and Peter rebuked the spirit of rejection tormenting him!

Suddenly he threw up his arms, and started weeping and praising God! Then he exploded in tongues, in his usual way, with a lot of emotion! Peter brought the interpretation! He hit Br. Verwey in the pit of his stomach, and said : "Do not reject and look down on yourself like this! You are a son of the most high God, do not despise yourself like this. Jesus paid the price for your redemption! You are not to despise yourself at all! When Lazarus the beggar sat in front of the rich man's gate, everybody looked at him with disgust, [he wept louder] and when the dogs came to lick his wounds, they said: 'You are just a beggar, a good for nothing! ' **But when Lazarus died, the angels came to carry him to the bosom of Father Abraham"**

Before Peter could finish the interpretation, I saw a vision: **I saw Jesus on his white horse.** OH! What a magnificent steed we are going to see, and follow! The white horse, was about eighteen to thirty inches higher than any horse I have ever seen, much higher than the big, big, Lipizzan horses they use in the circus! **The King Of Kings was in the saddle! With him was a multitude of people on horseback!**

Peter continued: **"When Our King, King Jesus comes on His white horse,** and the elect on horses , with Him, you will also be there, so don't despise yourself and deem yourself unworthy!"

The presence of the Lord was nearly too much to endure. All of us felt as though our flesh might just disintegrate! Then Br. Verwey said that he had seen the following vision, while he was still in their bedroom.

He saw a wall built with white stones ,[he had never been to Israel] in the wall was a closed gate. In front of the gate sat a beggar, wearing rags instead of clothes, and he had terrible sores all aver his body. While he was looking, he saw how thin ,underfed, scrounging dogs came to the beggar. The dogs started licking the wounds of the beggar. Because he was so depressed, and his leg was so painful, he thought that was how God saw him. A good for nothing, and a beggar! He had misunderstood totally what God meant!

Br. Verwey exploded in tongues again, Peter knew he had seen a vision. Peter told him to wait before sharing the vision, as a confirmation he wanted to tell him what he saw, before he told us! Peter said: "You saw something about Gethsemane, it is not quite clear what, but it definitely relates to Gethsemane! Even so, I do not have the interpretation"

Br. Verwey said that he had seen **something that looks like a stop-valve,** but it was fastened with a strong rusty chain. Then he saw two beautiful hands take hold of the chain to break the stop-valve loose. When it was loose, the hands started turning this stop-valve. He was using both his hands to turn to the right side. Then he said, a thick stream of water flowed out. Peter said to him, keep on doing what you are doing. He looked at the way he was turning, and exclaimed: **"I am not opening the stop-valve, I am closing it!"**

Peter answered: "It is not a stop-valve, it is an old fashioned oil press, and it is not water coming out, it is olive oil, symbolizing the Holy Spirit, that came forth by the pressure and agony of Jesus. He paid and bought not only for our redemption, but also the Gifts of the Holy Spirit. Br Verwey was not sure or convinced, he said he would pray about it, because it definitely looked like water to him.

Then Br. Verwey said that the interpretation was for Peter: **"God said, that there has been confusion about the gifts of the Holy Spirit. Many doctrines had robbed the Body of the Lord from moving in the gifts. People are tired of doctrines they are looking for reality,** and the Lord wants to use Peter to teach the body of the Lord about the reality of the Holy Spirit, and the gifts."

What a spiritual feast we had! It all started with the skirt I had to make! Fortunately I was like the son who said he would not go, but repented and went. How thankful I still am, that I was obedient. I am now teaching the body of the Lord about the reality of the gifts of the Holy Spirit.

My sincere desire is, that every person reading this book, will have a serious "stock-take" to determine if he or she, is enjoying the fullness of the gifts that Jesus paid such a dear price for! The strange tongues, the interpretation of tongues, visions, and all the other gifts mentioned in the Bible. **Why should you rob yourself** of some advantage **Jesus paid** for. If He, the Son of God thought it necessary, to such an extent that he was prepared to die to achieve that for us, **why should you allow anything or anybody to rob you?**

Let me finish, Br. Verwey has a very childlike faith. He told the Lord that he was not convinced that he saw olive oil, as Peter said, he was under the impression that it was water. He asked the Lord, to please put the stop-valve down in his lounge again, for him to verify if it was water or olive oil!Our great, big wonderful God, granted him his request, and he saw the stop-valve and stream again. In the Spirit, he put his finger into the stream, and smelled! It was definitely olive oil!

Dear reader, this is undoubtedly part of the last days. We will need every help we can possibly find, to remain standing, in the face of terrorism and tribulation. Claim it, it is available and paid for!

About three years later, a lady, the president of Women Aglow, came to visit us. We were sharing testimonies, and enjoying it tremendously! The Lord's presence was revealed to us !

She told us that she was seeing a strange stop-valve. She saw the same two hands taking hold of the chain, and saw the chain being broken, and saw that a stream of water gushed out. She too was turning in the wrong direction, Peter told her to continue turning. Once again, she found that she was closing, not opening. We told her then that she saw an old fashioned oil-press. She gave the same interpretation, that God wants to reveal the necessity of the gifts to His body. She said Peter and I was chosen by the Lord, to testify about the gifts of the Holy Spirit!

What an Amazing God we have! He is able to teach us through our understanding., or by His Spirit speaking to our spirit! The Lord is faithful and able to do far and exceedingly abundantly, above what we ask or think! Let us give Him our utmost, for His Highest possible price paid!

26

We decided to emigrate from South Africa. We went to Australia, to see if we would like to go there. We loved Brisbane, and we even found a house just like the one we had in SA. Another four families wanted to go with us, but we had to spy out the land first.

We were amazed at the freedom from crime there. People would go on vacation (holiday) in Australia, without locking their homes! Totally different from home! They left their cars unlocked at shopping malls! The change from our high tension living, was dramatic! We actually felt tired, because of the lack of tension., that cause an adrenalin flow! We foresaw the rise in crime in SA, and wanted to give our children a safer future.

Oh! The Gold Coast was so beautiful! It stretched and stretched for miles and miles! They had just started to develop the homes with waterways around it. Shopping by boat or by car! How exciting!

Friends of ours stayed in Gladstone, quite a ways from Brisbane, so, we rented a car to be able to see some of the country. What a disappointment it was. Eucalyptus trees, all the way! Peter, his logic mind working, said it made him realize how much work it would take to clear out land for farming. He told me to drive the most of the way! He kept his eyes closed, because it made him tired, to figure out who had to do all the work!.

We had the strangest experience of our lives in Gladstone! We had to meet our friend at his business, at a certain time. We got to his office at the set time, but the businesses and street was totally deserted. NO one in an open office! No one in any of the other open businesses! Had the rapture taken place? No, that could not be, because more will be left behind than would be taken, and what about us?! We walked, looked and called into offices, and then drove around in a daze! Absolutely no sign of life! Not a single solitary soul to be seen! We saw the road signs to the airport! AH! we would go there! Maybe we could find a solution there!

At the airport, **No One around!** The offices were open, baggage standing around, as though forsaken, even the till was not closed! Peter walked to one of the planes on the runway, he banged on the plane and called out loudly: **"Anyone Here, Please answer me!** "Nothing! OH! It sure felt eerie! What on earth was going on? Had a strange gas killed all? But No, we did not see any dead person, just emptiness! Wow! We were extremely puzzled! **What were we to do? Where do we go to?**

We drove back to town. **NO car or person was moving!** Strange sensation! What was going on? NO, why was anything NOT going on? By then we had fallen silent. Each busy with our own questions!

Suddenly! In a corner shop, **a Living person moved!** What a relief! Peter just about ran in! He asked the man, very agitatedly and urgently, where all the people were, what on earth was wrong? **The man burst out laughing,** he screamed with laughter! When at last he could control himself, he said: **"Obviously you are a stranger to our town, You will not find anybody, anywhere, today, they are all on the sports grounds! We have our annual sports,** bazaar, rugby, games, competitions, the crowning of our beauty queen, **and ALL is there,** nobody misses the fun! Even the planes are scheduled to fly in or out before, or after the events! What a big relief, the mystery was solved! Fortunately we could get something to eat and drink at his shop!

We had a nice visit with our friend, and were very glad to fly back to Brisbane, it was so much quicker and easier, than having to drive!

Back in Brisbane, we visited an Assemblies of God Church. It was a very big congregation, and **they invited everybody present in the meeting** that morning, **to a wedding and a reception,** that evening. I said to Peter, to have about 3,000 people to attend a wedding reception! I have to experience that! In South Africa, the Mother and Father of the bride have to see to everything, all the food, and the drinks.

How expensive, to cater for the whole assembly! **I had to see, and experience that!**

At the evening service, all, were invited to attend the wedding! We moved to the hall, and saw that **every family brought cake, cooked meat, salads, drinks, juice, chips or whatever they wanted to bring. Soon, all the tables were FULL of delicious food!** Everyone joined in the festivity, and there were food, and food and more food! Within an hour, we were all full and overflowing, literally and spiritually! Then the good part! **Each person helped to clear and clean up,** within a record time the hall was clean and neat. All could leave, happy, not overworked, just overindulged! WOW I wish the people at home would adopt that way of celebrating a wedding, then all can be part of the blessing, giving and receiving!

We decided to carry on with our plans to emigrate. Every thing was going well, when one day a "brother" came to see us. We had kept our plans very quiet, not wanting anyone to interfere. He told us that he had a "Word" from God for us. I did not feel free to accept what he had to say. Peter wanted to know from him, if he knew anything about our plans. He compressed his lips, to a big NOOOO! Shaking his head vehemently! So he started with me. He said the Lord told him, that I wanted to go to Australia. It is a strange country, with strange customs, and strange people, and I would not be happy there. Why do I want to go there, and what do I want to find there. He went on, and on and he convinced Peter, but not me. I did not accept what he said, but because Peter was the head, and he stopped the proceedings to go to Australia, I had to submit.

Our life just fell apart! We started losing money, and everything went wrong. On a Saturday morning my daughter, Carise, her husband and their two little girls, the eldest, Fine', my namesake, and the little one Lize came to our home. I have never, ever been jealous of my children's friends, and had never tried to keep them apart. However, that morning, as soon as I saw them, an inexpressible, groundless, obsession took hold of me! **I did not want my daughter near a friend**

of hers. I wanted to keep them as far apart as the North pole is, from the South.

I said to her, Please don't go to your friend today. She said to me: "Why, I haven't seen her for about three weeks. Of course I am going to see her! What's wrong with you, Mom?" I was helpless, floundering, I did not know why I felt like I did, but it was an obsession with me. She got annoyed with me, so they left.

When they got home, her friend, husband and little son was awaiting their return. They all went to my son in law's brother for the day. At about four thirty, they decided that they all would spend the evening at Carise's home. The two ladies went ahead, Carise driving her friend's car.

A drunken driver, skipped the robot when my daughter was turning, slammed into the friends car, a few inches behind the right front door. Little Lize was sitting on the friend's lap, and the terrible blow hurled her against the front panel. Carise and her friend cut their heads against each other from the jolt. The two men, who left a little later, were the first on the scene after the accident! They called the police, but my son in law took Carise, the baby and their friend, who was pregnant to the hospital.

About five o'clock, my son in law called. He said there had been an accident, my daughter and the baby were in hospital, and we had better come quickly!

Because we experienced having a mentally disabled child, I asked my son Karel, to phone our prayer chain. He had to tell them to ask God, that should Lize have brain damage, that He have to take her home! We quickly drove to the hospital.

As we walked into the hospital, we passed the emergency room. The door was slightly ajar, and I saw little Lize on the table, with a few doctors around her. As I looked I saw her little hand going up, then saw how it fell limply backwards in an unnatural way. **I knew then, she had passed away.** Oh, Dear God! **How to face my daughter?!** How to tell her the awful news? How much more steep will the painful road get?

We went to my daughter, she was bleeding, her face was cut, and she was in terrible pain. Her shoulder bone was broken, and she had a bit of concussion, and bruises all over. The doctor called us out of the room, and told us that little Lize, had passed away! He suggested that we should not tell Carise, but I said, that we had to tell her, because it would be bad for her, to have another shock, later again.

Peter and I, accompanied by the doctor, went to Carise. Her Dad and I held her hands, and told her that Lize had gone to be with the Lord. OH, the heartrending pain! She started crying and weeping like a mortally wounded little animal. She was still sobbing, and crying, when the sweet Holy Spirit took over. **Rom. 8.26 "We do not know what we ought to pray for, but the Spirit Himself intercedes for us, with groans that words cannot express** Carise, groaned and screamed, in tongues. The broken, abject, searing agony, was being torn and wrenched from her. Deep, Oh, deep the valley. Steep, so steep the mountain! For her to climb that mountain, unaided, was impossible, and for me too! We needed, and had a hand to hold onto, the Lord's **Psm: 94. 17 "UNLESS the Lord had given me help, I would soon have dwelt in the silence of death. 18. When I said, my foot is slipping, Your love, O Lord, supported me.19. When anxiety was great within me, Your consolation brought joy to my soul!"**

The doctor was standing by, with a syringe to put her to sleep, but we motioned to him not to do that. He looked on, but could not understand the praying in tongues. The Lord had him wait patiently, until after about ten minutes, Carise started weeping softly, then she asked the doctor, to bring her the little one, to hold her for the last time, to say her farewell to her little girl. She said, as she held her, at first she had not wanted her, so soon after Fine', and just when she started to love her, she's gone. Without the opportunity to get to know her.

OH! Don't Delay! Let's love Today! She was only ten and a half months old, so young, so small! When would it be your turn, or my turn to go? Where are you heading? I have more than One reason, to want to go to Jesus! Many dear people whom I love, are waiting for me there!

I tried to console Carise in the days after Lize went to Jesus, but I have to admit and confess, I was totally inadequate. I had NO knowledge of the pain, and agony, of losing one of your own children! Dear reader, if you have not been there, let me assure you, there is NO way that you could even remotely identify with the pain of losing a child! OH! What Pain! Far, far worse than the Pain I had in my stomach was the pain in our hearts! Steep, surely, a very steep road! (I had no idea, that I had to climb that mountain at a later stage!)

27

Peter was not fond of answering the phone, but I was busy preparing lunch, when the phone rang. I asked him to get it, because I was busy. He came back with a puzzled look on his face, asking me if I knew anyone on a town, Middelburg, about 450 miles from us. I said No. He told me there was a strange person on the phone, wanting to speak to Fine.

When I answered, the person, a man, asked if it was Fine' speaking. I said yes, it is me. He said Praise the Lord! (Loudly) He then said while he was praying the night before, the Lord told him to phone me,and **the Lord gave him my phone number and name! Imagine that!** Obviously, I got very excited!

I said to him: "You surely must have a message for me, if God gave you my number and name!" (I always want to hear from Him!) He answered: "Yes I do have a message for you. Do you know a Martie human?"

I thought this over for a while, and said to him I might know somebody by that name, but what is it all about? He said: **"The Lord told me that Martie Human wants to enlarge their home, but they do not have the money they need to do it, and I have to give her R500"** I was somewhat taken aback, because I thought the message would be for me, about me!. Now it had other consequences as well.

However, I told him that it gives me pleasure to do what the Lord wants, and that I would give Martie the R500. **Every sentence he spoke was punctuated by a loud: Praise The Lord!** When he spoke to Peter, he did the same.

I asked him for his telephone number, but he said they did not have a telephone, he phoned from somebody else. His name was Pieter de Wet, and they were only living for a short while in Middelburg, from where he phoned. Before I could ask for another phone number to contact him, the line went dead. I do not know if maybe, it was an angel or not. I tried various ways to reach him, to no avail!

Peter and I, were dumbfounded! Can you Imagine, the wonders of God! Sure, we say that he lives in our hearts, but I had never thought that He would have somebody call on my name, and with our telephone number! **Miraculous! Absolutely Miraculous!**

My search for Martie Human started. The lady I thought to Martie had another surname! Peter said he was not all too eager to give the money away. I had better make sure to find the right person. **I often called her name out Loudly**, asking her to get in contact with me, since I did not know where to find her. I asked the Lord to tell me where to find her. A few weeks passed. One morning I was on the first floor of our home, I thought Peter was out. I called again, Loudly, telling Martie Human to please contact me! Peter came in and told me to stop this nonsense, I must not call again.

A while later, early in the morning, I had a very big urgency to clean my home. My daughter Carise asked me why I was in such a hurry. I did not know, but **as Always Jesus knew**. I was just finished, when the phone rang.

When I answered, the lady who called, was apologetic for phoning so early. I asked who she was, and, she said I would probably not even remember her. I saw her only twice at our friend Ria Scherman's house, her name is Martha. Sure I remembered her. She said she needed counseling, and would be grateful if I could pray for her. She decided to come over immediately, I realized, that this visit, was the cause of the hasty home cleaning!

Martha came and we shared some testimonies. She then complained that she did not really see and experience answers to her prayers, even though she walked closely with the Lord. They also had financial problems. Every time when it seemed things would be better, their car, the washing machine, or something else would break. This caused them to be in the red continually. She asked me to pray for answered prayers and finances.

Peter and I prayed for her, then, he had to leave. She said she should also be leaving, but she had a burning desire to share a testimony with me. She told me, that ever since they came to South Africa from Namibia, they had wanted to enlarge the very small kitchen of their home. However, the problem was, they had no funds. Her husband wanted to make a loan from the bank, but she discouraged him, saying if they did not have the money, where would they find money to pay back the loan plus interest.

They decided to make it a prayer priority. Her husband, two daughters and herself asked the Lord, to please supply the funds to enlarge their small kitchen, if it was His will. A few days thereafter, somebody called her husband at work. This person would not give his name, he told Johan, her husband that the Lord told him, the caller, that he needed a present, but he did not want to disclose what type of present. He said it would be delivered to their home the following day! Of course, they were very anxious to find out what the secret present was!

The next day, a truckload of building sand, and a truckload of concrete stone were delivered. The driver of the truck did not know who sent it, only that it was already paid for. Thereafter, they dug the foundations for the enlargement of the kitchen! Every time he drove somewhere, he stopped at building sites, asked for the unused bricks and started building. I was listening intently, praising God all the time.

But, now, she said, their finances, all the sand, the concrete, and the cement were finished, and the walls were only finished to just under the roof. There was no way they could complete the kitchen.

Suddenly my mind was electrified, renewed! I asked her:" Martha, what is your surname?" She seemed surprised, she said: "MY surname, Why?" I said; "Please tell me, what is your surname?" **"My surname is Human, why do you want to know?"** she said. I started laughing and laughing, I said to her:**"You say that you do not really See answers to your prayers, that is a very Big Joke!"** She could not understand what was happening. **I told her about the phone call** from far away, **how God gave him her name** my name and also my phone number. She sat quite still, her mouth hanging open, her arms hanging down next to the chair, I waited for her reaction, at last she said: "Do you mean to tell me I came here today to get the money?"

I said: "Yes surely you came here to fetch the money. I have been calling you for weeks to come!" She started laughing, she said: "Three weeks ago I was praying and weeping before the Lord, asking for money to finish the kitchen. The Lord told me to come to you. I told Him that you would not even remember me, why should I come to you. Two weeks ago, I was praying again, and the Lord told me once more to come to you, but I had the same excuse.

This morning I was really totally desperate, I wept before Him, then **He shouted** to me **"Go To Fine'** "I got so frightened, I jumped up, phoned, and asked Ria for your phone number. **Do you mean to tell me, I have been crying and asking unnecessarily for the money for three whole weeks?!"** (How often don't we do just that!) She left on cloud nine, she had the check for R500! They could finish their kitchen supernaturally!

Late that afternoon, I was cutting some sheets for my daughter, Carise, when the doorbell rang. Elna opened the door, while I stayed down on the floor to finish the cutting. Martie and her husband came in, and I invited them to sit, I just had to cut a short way. She said they just came because he wanted to thank us for the money. I was disconcerted, I told them it was the Lord's doing, not mine.

She talked , but he sat staring at me, and I felt a little uneasy, because many people seems to see something otherwise, or strange about me! Eventually, he said to her: "Darling, do you remember the vision of a woman I saw, while I was on the scaffolding?" She said: "Yes I remember, but what about her?'

"Well, this is the woman I saw at that time."(Pointing at me)

I had never met Johan before that day. He then told me, that when he was using his last bit of material, he told the Lord that everything was totally finished. He asked the Lord how they would be able to finish. Suddenly he saw a vision of a woman with dark blond hair, and blue eyes. The Lord told him that the woman he saw in the vision, would give them the money to finish!

He climbed down, and asked Martie if she has a friend with dark blond hair and blue eyes. Martie laughed and said that she has quite a number of friends who could be the one he mentioned. She asked him why he was asking about this lady. He said to her: "My wife, the Lord has just told me, that lady will give us the money to finish building!"

Now here is another lesson! She had been praying and weeping for money, but when he said that the Lord showed him the lady who would give them money she said: "OH, My poor darling, it must be your imagination, you are over stressed. Who on earth will give US money?"

The Lord removed the little discrepancy about Martie and Martha, by him having the vision of me, just to show us without a shadow of a doubt, the testimony is absolutely true!

They definitely had a stumbling block. NO MONEY! Jesus changed the stumbling block into a stepping stone, not only for them, but also to have you and I know that **nothing is impossible with God!**

28

At the time Peter and I became Spirit filled Christians, I did not know a lot of ministries, one of the few I knew about was Oral Roberts. A friend had some tapes of his conference meetings. I longed to do exploits for the Lord but did not know how. I told the Lord that it was not my fault that I was born on a farm, and that I was a woman. Women did not play a very big role in ministry in South Africa, at that time.

As I was telling the Lord about this, He showed me in a vision a little ground dam we had when I was a child. It was the main source of pleasure to a very lonely little girl. I found a cylinder type of thing, with many openings, just what I needed! I used to throw this cylinder into the dam, wait till the water became clear, then watch how the different kinds of frogs, would find shelter in this cylinder. After some time, I would run into the dam, take the cylinder and throw it out on the ground.

This was what it was all about! I would count how many frogs I had caught, not to kill them, Oh!No! They were precious! I was competing against myself, day after day. I think my top score were 14 frogs. You might ask, what has that to do with my desire to do things for Jesus?

The Lord showed me, in the vision that little dam, it then existed only in my spirit, because it had long since been filled up. I saw a hand pick up a stone, and throw it into the middle of the dam. In the vision, I heard the plunge and saw the circles, circling out, ever wider, till it covered, and came to the very edge of the dam! The Lord said: **"If you remain true to Me, I will cause your testimonies, about Me, to go all over the world, just as you see the circles going out ever wider till It reaches the end of the dam!"**

I have testified wherever I went, but I think it might be a fitting time, to tell you more about the: BLOOD OF JESUS.

The church my parents and I were members of, mentioned the Blood of Jesus only in a perfunctory way. Therefore, when I came in contact with Spirit filled Christians, and heard so much talk about the Blood of Jesus, I wanted to know what it really meant. I asked Him to make it clear to me, in a way I would understand. I had also heard of some that had seen visions of Jesus, and had a desire to be able to see Him too.

While I was praying, He showed me Himself on the cross. **He looked at me, and I knew, with absolute certainty, that HE knew EVERYTHING about me. There was Nothing I could even try to hide** from His Loving eyes, He was looking straight into my soul. And, do you know what? **Even though He knew everything, He still loved ME!** OH! It was more than I could handle! I felt so ashamed of all the wrong things I did, I had an overpowering desire to make good! **The price for me was so awesome! I was so unworthy** and Still Am!

Writing about this brings it SO vividly back. I can but weep and say: **"I am yours Lord! Use me, change me, make me over anew! If this clay fails, do not throw me away, please, make me into Your own vessel!**

In the vision, I saw that He looked down, and I saw a brown wooden coffin. I knew it was my coffin and I was in the coffin! Then, **Oh! great merciful Jesus! A drop from where the thorns had pierced his brow, a drop of the Blood of the King of Kings, fell onto my coffin!**

As soon as His blood touched the coffin, it started to spread. It covered all of my coffin. **The coffin changed wherever the blood flowed, and became white as snow, as far as the blood spread, until the whole coffin was totally white!**

OH! How many, many times did I thank the dear Lord for that vision! I was still in my first love, I had discarded many of the old baggage, the old sins, and thought patterns. I was definitely sure

that I "qualified" for heaven. Later, I had to learn the hard, hard way, that I was just at the beginning of the training. I often rejoice because I am sure, that the cleansing flow shall continually do all that is needed, till at death. Oh! Hallelujah! I am headed towards heaven! HIS BLOOD will never ever lose Power!

29

After the death of my little granddaughter, things got totally out of hand. Peter and I could not make sense out of life. We prayed and asked the Lord to reveal and speak to us, that we might know. We were pastors of a Church, and I invited brother and sister Verwey to come to our church, and to have lunch with us afterward. I realized that he has a very unique gift of visions, and I hoped that the Lord would show him something about us., but Peter knew nothing about this.

We ladies, admire bone china. **Do you know why it is called Bone China?** In China, they eat a lot of pork. All the bones are thrown into a quarry, and mixed with ground. **The pig bones** wear away and **becomes part of the ground**, after a long time. The potters then use this Bone Ground to make the most expensive Bone China teacups and dinnerware.

This Bone Ground needs a lot of kneading, much, much more than ordinary ground. This pig-bone dirt, does not lie still on the potter's wheel easily. After the kneading process, it has to be flung down, with great might, onto the potter's wheel. Often quite a few times, before it would become submissive,can be formed into something exquisite. Sometimes, it has to be kneaded all over again, before being flung onto the wheel yet again. I have an idea, that maybe I was formed out of such pig-bone ground!

Saturday night, while Peter and I prayed together, he had a Word of Knowledge. He said to me: **"I can't understand why, but I Know** brother & sister Verwey will be in church with us tomorrow, even though they do not worship at our assembly. **He is going to see a vision,** then **he will speak in tongues, and God will give me the interpretation. The, interpretation will clarify our situation,** and help us to realize, what is happening in our lives." I did not tell him that I had invited them, therefore, I knew he was speaking the truth.

In church, we sang a few choruses, when suddenly brother Verwey exploded in tongues, with much passion and verve. Peter, had the same passion and verve in the interpretation. I do not have the tape with me now, but will recount basically, verbally what the Lord said, with the help of the Holy Spirit.

"**There are three stages of worship** for a child of God. **The first stage** is when **God, the Potter takes you, a useless lump** of clay, out of the ground. Then God pours the water of the Holy Spirit on you, and kneads, and kneads you, till you are pliable. When you are pliable, He throws you onto the potter's wheel. **The Master Potter,** then, **forms something beautiful and useful** out of the useless lump of clay.

"When the clay (You and Me) realizes that it was changed and has now become beautiful and useful, it starts to praise and worship the Potter. This worship is very acceptable and pleasing to God." Tongues again, this is the interpretation:

"Unfortunately, when the clay realizes that it has become beautiful and useful, pride enters into the clay. Pride, cannot be condoned by the potter, because it is harmful to the clay. Therefore, even though it pains the Potter, He has to break the vessel he made. **It is extremely painful** for the clay **to be broken** into fragments, thus, to become unlovely and useless again. **However, If the clay in this broken situation, recognizes** that **it was broken because of pride,** and starts to worship, **in the brokenness, worship the Potter, That** is even more acceptable and pleasing to the potter. It is more precious than the worship of the first stage. **"This is the second stage of worship"** Tongues again:

"The clay has to realize fully, that the Potter has the supreme say. It has to remain humble, remembering without doubt, that it is totally dependent on the potter. **When the clay becomes willing to yield and to submit** to the potters hand completely, **only then will the potter make something of the clay again!.**" This then, is **the third stage** of praise and worship. **This is the most acceptable and pleasing praise and worship to offer the Great Potter!** I stand, **I stand , in Awe of You!**

Psm 5.7 "But as for me I will worship toward, and at Your holy temple IN reverent fear and awe of YOU Psm. 51.10 'Create in me a clean heart, O God; and renew a right, persevering and steadfast spirit in me!" Verse **17 "My sacrifice (the sacrifice acceptable) to God is a broken and a contrite heart** (broken down with sorrow for sin and humbly and thoroughly penitent) **such O God, You will not despise."**

How long, how very long, did it take this piece of clay to come to the third stage of worship! OH! Great Potter, Jesus, Thank you so much for your patience with me! All my confusion He understood, all I have to offer Him is brokenness, and strife, but He makes something beautiful of my life! That is my sincere hope and desire!

30

We were on tour in London with a group of seventeen Christians. We had heard of people on fire for the Lord. Therefore we wanted to meet them, so we phoned them. They told us they would meet us at a certain station. We liked to travel on the underground, it was a nice new experience for us, because we do not have that in SA. They came to fetch us, with a very small little bus. During the ride I was afraid that I would not be able to untangle my legs from the others again!

On the street corner were two young men, eating ice cream cones. One of them saw the fourteen heads, in this extremely small space. (Some of the group did not come.) He was so amazed, he nearly swallowed his ice cream whole, while he nudged his mate and kept pointing at us!

The meeting, was in a very large room, about sixty to a hundred people were gathered there. We did not know how they worshiped, and they probably felt the same about us. There was a kind of tenseness, so, Peter said we should give each other a hug, introduce ourselves, and pray for each other!

OH! MY! That was like the word: GO! Everybody got in motion, hugging and greeting, and not silently either! I went to two ladies, put my arms around both, said Hello, and prayed for them. When one lady fell over, I was totally caught by surprise! I knelt by her, laid my hands on her and prayed in my own language, it was certainly like tongues to her. I said to the Lord, that I did not know what she needed, or what the matter was with her. If she was sick, that He should heal her completely, and do whatever she needs. After a while I helped her to get up, and she jumped (I nearly said flew) to the other lady, they took hold each other tightly, hugged and cried! I thought, O, well, I'll leave them, let them carry on praising the Lord.

As soon as I started to move away, the other lady caught my coat and pulled me closer. She said: "Do you know what the Lord has just done for this lady?" I said: "No, I don't." She said: "The Lord has just opened her eyes! She has been blind for eleven years!" I was overcome with praise! A man was just entering the room, and before I could reply, the now seeing lady, started yelling! "Jimmy, JIMMY! I can see! JIMMY! I can see, I can see!" The three of them got hold of each other and started praising God! Tears and sweat mingled! Jimmy was wearing a dark blue sports jacket, and soon he had sweat patches showing under his arms! Their joy was exceedingly great, and they were not ashamed to show it!

We prayed for other young people, and the Lord baptized the one after the other in the Holy Spirit. As soon as we prayed for one person, and he or she spoke in tongues, another would say; "I also want that!" What a memorable evening! **What a "Memorable God" we serve!**

From England we flew to Geneva, in Switzerland. Whenever I think of Switzerland I always remember how extremely clean every thing was. We stayed in a hotel near the big lake. The reflection of the lights on the water had us spellbound, especially when they had the fountain spouting. It shoots up the water, maybe a hundred or two hundred feet in the air! The year before, Peter, and I, and our sons, Karel and Jakes, were there, so we could tell the others about the best sights to see!

The next morning, we left the hotel by bus, at half past five. The mist was so heavy, that the bus had to crawl along, visibility was just at about nil! We had experienced the same situation the year before, and because of the mist, we were unable to go up the mountain with the cable car. Because I knew that, I told the group that we had to pray, to ask God to remove the mist, or it would be a wasted day. However, they did not realize the urgency of the situation, so, I went to the front of the bus, borrowed the mike from the driver, and told them in Afrikaans (our Language) to close their eyes and mouths, **I wanted to pray!**

The Lord Graciously granted our request, because a few miles down the road, the mist looked liked finger curtains that was being drawn up! By the time we reached the little town Chamonix, the day was exquisitely beautiful and crystal clear! **OH! What a day!** We went up the mountain with the cable car. WAW! The view and **ride to the top was exhilarating!** (It means: to set aglow with happiness or elation, to make cheerful) How beautiful Heaven will be, if God created earth so fabulously pretty!

We were indeed cheerful, and aglow with happiness! It was indescribably awesome, to see how beautiful and majestic the mountains were! We ate snow, built snowmen, made snowballs threw each other, chased around and played like children all day long. What a joyous day we had! How wonderful it is to enjoy LIFE in the presence of the Lord. **In HIM we live and move and have our being.** Too often we kind of behave, as though we need to be SOO austere, prim and proper! I like to jump, and praise the Lord! All the time!

In the bus on our way back to Geneva, I said to Peter, **I would like to go to church,** because we had not yet met any Christians, and were leaving for Italy the next morning. Peter said it already was more than twelve hours since we left the Hotel that morning, and he was very tired. He said I could go, if I wanted to, as much as I wanted to, I just had to allow him to rest. We had dinner, and after dinner, Peter and I went to our bedroom. I needed to organize our luggage and pack for our flight the next morning.

Soon somebody knocked, it was Andre, a sturdy young man, and part of our group. He asked me to come with him to pray for Grandpa. The old man was already 84, and he had remained in the hotel that day, because of a bad bout of flue. I went with him to their room. I prayed for Grandpa, then while someone else prayed for him, I saw a vision.

In the vision I saw a woman in a small apartment (flat) Her apartment was very artistically decorated. There were flowers and other beautiful hanging decorations. The lady was standing in front of the zinc, in her apartment's small kitchenette. She was staring out through the window. This lady had a severe longing for God, the longing was so great, that it actually became a physical pain. The Lord told me to come in contact with this Lady. I said, BUT, LORD, (Too often I do that!) where will I find her? Geneva is an extremely big city. If You, Lord, do not help me to find her, where do I start? (I thought about going to church again.)

Then the Lord wrote a few French words for me in the vision. I laughed, I said: "Lord Jesus, I do not know as much about French as a French Poodle, I do not even know how to chase a poodle away in French!"

After prayer, I went to Irene, she was our help, because she knew the basics in French. I asked her if she could read the French words? She said: "I can read them, but it is far too difficult for me, way beyond my understanding! **I'm afraid I do not have a clue what it means!**" I told her, that I wanted to go to reception, to find out about a church, also that I would ask them the meaning of the words.

At reception, I asked the one young girl, if there was a Pentecostal Church near the hotel. She said: "Pentecostal, what is that?" I said: "Well, it is a church where the people clap their hands." They laughed and giggled behind their hands, and then one came up with a solution! "Yes, Madame, if you would go down to the lake, catch bus number ??, go to bus stop number ??, catch bus number ??, it will stop near a church like that."I answered her in Afrikaans, waving my hands in a negative fashion, while shaking my head: 'No thank you, this lady will not be able to go there, and find my way back.' Now for the next question!

I showed her the French words, she read them, and I asked her if she understood what she read. Her eyes were big, as she looked at me, she said she understood the words. she said: **"This is wonderful, words,** magnificent words, but **my English not very good, I cannot tell you what it means**" That, was THAT! I could not find a church, I did not know what the French words meant, so my mission was in vain!

As I walked towards the door, I heard some hasty conversation behind me, while I grumbled: **"Mission uncompleted, Lord!"** A dark sturdy, swarthy man came quickly to me and said: **"Madame, can I be of assistance to you?** I can speak English as well as French?" OH! My Goodness!! **He was extremely theatrical** in his way of talking, he made elaborate signs with his hands. He would hold his thumb and middle finger together, the other three fingers outstretched! He talked with an accent, like an Arab or Pakistani. I was more than a little over-awed by him, **so I asked him** meekly, **if he knew of a church Nearby the hotel!** He said in his exuberant way: (meaning: abounding in high spirits and vigor; full of joy and vigor, overflowing and lavish!) Lavish! That describes him very aptly!) **"AH, Yes Madame!** As a matter of fact, **there is a church just a few blocks from the hotel I can take you there now, Madame, if you will come with me!"**

What! I did not want to end up in a harem! I thought quickly. I told him I had to tell my husband first. **I needed to tell Peter** that I was going with him. However my need was not so much to tell Peter, **my intention was to ASK Andre, to accompany me,** as I did not desire to go out into the night, with the stranger by myself! He might have the wrong reasons, to take me out! OH! NO! **Thank you, but no thank you!**

Before he could go further, I asked him if he was able to read the French words. He looked at the words, and his demeanor became even more exuberant and theatrical. He Exclaimed: **"This is wonderful words. magnificent words! But where did you get these words?"** (OH! NO! He sounded like an echo of the girls!) Meekly pointing to heaven, I said: **"Well, I got them from the Lord,** but can **you tell ME what it means?"** With hands and fingers and his whole body adding strength to his serious theatrical answer, **he said: "It means you will be supernaturally refreshed by GOD!"**

Well, Well, that was a really fantastic interpretation! At that time I did not realize, precisely HOW spot on it was, or how timely the supernatural refreshing, by God!

The stranger was waiting for my answer, so, I told him, I wanted to go to tell my husband that I was going to the church with him. Also that I would meet him at reception, in ten minutes. I quickly went to tell Peter, then to fetch Andre to accompany me.

We met the dramatic stranger, and the walk saga started! Up one block, down the other, up the next block, down the other. Not a single church, could be found! He was very, very apologetic, and sorry, but could not understand why he could not find the church, he definitely saw it that morning! After more than an hour, I told him that I was tired, we had been on the mountain the whole day. I have always given him the benefit of the doubt, because of what happened after the walk.

When I got to our bedroom, Peter was very unhappy with the situation. He said he was tired and wanted to rest. I played for time, because God does not lie, neither has He time to waste. I packed our bags, and got the clothes ready for the next day. Peter admonished me. He said: "I know your tactics all too well. You are playing for time, and I can tell you now, if God wants you to meet this woman, He will send her to your room! (not our room!) Get into bed now, I want to sleep! NOW this moment!" Somebody knocked! It was Andre. He said: "Please Aunt Fine', could you come to help me? When I got out of the lift (elevator) a lady was standing there, with a dog. I handed her a tract,and she exclaimed!

"Can you tell me more about the Holy Spirit? Oh! I Need to know More About the Holy Spirit please tell me more about the Holy Spirit!? "I took her to our bedroom, but my English is not very good. Will you please come to talk to the lady? **"Of Course!** I was more than willing and eager to do that. **Here was the lady of the vision, God did send her to me!** I was so happy to oblige!

We went to their bedroom, but I realized that Grandpa, who was sick, needed rest. Without further thought, I suggested we should go to our bedroom. So, we went to our room. However, the moment I put the key into the lock, I realized my mistake! Inside was a tremendously tired man! But, it was too late, I could not retrace my steps, so I opened the door! lo! and! behold! Can you guess? **Who, had been supernaturally refreshed BY GOD! My husband, Peter!**

He was sitting in bed! It looked as though he wanted to say. "Come into my parlor" like the spider said to the fly! **He was ready to minister to the lady.** She then said to us, **she really needed to hear** about the Holy Spirit. **Unfortunately,** she would not be able to listen. **Her dog got sick** in her apartment, and started vomiting. She took him for a walk, she meant to go to the lake, **but he pulled her into the hotel.** She thought he wanted to visit her friend, who was staying on the same floor as Andre. However, they were there for only a few minutes, when he started scratching at the door and wanted to get out.

You guessed correctly! **God's timing was perfect** to the second! **As Andre got out** of the elevator, (lift) **she was there, waiting!** I cannot endorse enough, how **My Heavenly Father does hear and answer** when we call! **She had the desperate desire to know more about the Holy Spirit! She must have called** on the Lord, **that is why I saw the vision, and the strange words. Then the strange man, the long walk, everything worked together for good**, to get Andre at the elevator at exactly the right time! It was the Lord's, split second timing!

"She said, "unfortunately" [no, by divine appointment] her dog got sick and therefore she will not be able to listen to us. HA! HA! I bent down, stroked the doggy, and prayed in my own language. I said to the Lord, HE wanted us to contact the lady, **would HE please put this dog to sleep!** Just like He put Adam to sleep, before He removed a rib, to create Eve? Within minutes the dog snored, deep even, peaceful snores. She was amazed! **Never ever**, she said, in all of his life, **has her dog snored!** It was the first time she has ever heard him snore!

She was a very clever lady. She did translating, at the United Nations. She could speak, read and write seven languages. As usual, **Peter, was doing all the talking, after my walking!** I always did the groundbreaking work, then he did the nice part, the actual sowing. **Peter and I, mostly he, shared with her, and prayed with and for her.** She told us, that her mother taught her, if she needed advice or wisdom, to pray and ask God to speak to her, then to open the Bible! She said **it always amazed her how accurate the answers were. I could sincerely agree with her!**

It was nearly twelve o'clock, when Andre and I walked with her to her apartment. I lost her name and address, with the bible I wrote it in, so if maybe she reads this testimony, God Bless you Abundantly! If you could contact me, even better! Otherwise, it will be another unfinished Symphony, to be concluded in Heaven! OH! I look forward to hear all the conclusions! Do YOU doubt it? I Don't, the word says: **MICAH 4.4 "But they shall sit every (wo)man under his/her vine and under his/her fig tree, and none shall make them afraid; for the mouth of the Lord of Hosts has spoken it."** There will be no one who will say: "I would like to listen to you, BUT I don't have the time!" We will have eternity to thank HIM, praise HIM and tell of HIS wondrous works of love for us!

31

A pastor, Len, started ministering in a tent. He invited us to come to help him. Peter, told him that we definitely would not come, unless he made good provision for our accommodation! Three of our kids were to accompany us, Carise, Karel and Jakes. Pastor Len replied that he had arranged a Seven Star type accommodation, it was ready and waiting for our arrival.

We drove for four to five hours to this ministry and "Accommodation". We arrived shortly before sunset, to find a very, very small caravan, suitable for only two people, waiting for the five of us. When one person stood, in the caravan, four had to lie down. The outlook was a bit bleak! The caravan was bad news, but what was worse, was the ramshackle outside toilet we were supposed to use! As I told you before, a dubious outside toilet is my **nemesis.** This, I could and would not endure!

Soon, after we arrived, it was time for the service to start in the tent, about thirty paces away from our caravan. The three kids cried, and told me they were too tired after the long drive, to attend the church. I succumbed, in motherly love, hoping to put them to sleep, and then to slip away. Ah! No! They would not go to sleep, they sang choruses with the people in the tent, and had a roaring time! I was frustrated!

When the service was over, and the people ministered to, it was already late, before we could try to get some sleep. The tent was only few hundred yards from the border between South Africa, and Lesotho. Many black Sothos, passed our "Accommodation". Most of them came from parties and were drunk, they sang and talked loudly in their own language. Peter and I, were definitely not impressed. The kids slept soundly, while we were on guard.

As usual, my three early birds, needed to go to the nemesis, and were tired of being in bed. There was but one thing to do! I dressed them, loaded them into the Volkswagen Kombi (van), and went to the park. The kids enjoyed this tremendously! This was unusual fun **for them! not for me!** Just about nine o'clock, we went, to the tent." It rhymes, but in my mind, nothing rhymed. When we got to the caravan, Peter and the pastor were waiting for breakfast. I called the pastor's wife, pointed to a house nearby, and said to her, that **I have claimed that house for our own use. I wanted us to be able to use the bathroom and the toilet there.**

Because she is a very soft-spoken lady, she touched my arm gently. **She told me** that the people living in the house nearby, belonged to the traditional church, and therefore **we would not be able to use their home. I told her** that was nonsense, **I had already claimed that home.** While we were speaking, a car stopped at the gate. A lady got out and came to me. She asked me if I was the pastor of the tent's wife. I told her Christine was the one she should talk to.

She told Christine, they were going away for the weekend, but **she brought us the key** to their home. **She wanted us to use the bathroom, and the toilet,** and should we so desire, we could prepare food in her kitchen! She even offered that we could sleep there! **My heavenly Father knows, just what I need!** OH how sweet is His provision when we call on Him!

Whenever, I went to our **"special"** house, **I smelled** the abominable **fumes of tobacco!** I rebuked the tobacco devil and asked the Lord to clear and clean the house! Also to set the person who smoked absolutely free. I prayed that everyone who came into that house would come under conviction of sin.

After lunch, Peter and Len needed to prepare, and rest before the evening service. My three musketeers, plus the daughter of pastor Len, did not feel inclined to rest. So, off we went **to the park again!**

Before the evening service, my three kids tried the same tactics as the night before. That night, I was definitely not to be overruled. They could stay, by themselves, or go to church, there were only two choices. After quite a bit of bickering, they decided to go to church, because they were not brave enough to stay by themselves!

In the tent, I suddenly had aches and pains all over my body. My neck was so painful, I could not hold my head up. My back ached in more than one place, my legs felt as though they belonged to someone else. My knees were extremely sore, and I had a headache, deep behind my eyes, just to name a few of the problems.

Pastor Len told the congregation that we came from Johannesburg to help him. I did not feel able or capable to help anybody, and I hoped no one would look I my direction, I felt too bad!

He preached a powerful sermon, that all have sinned and gone astray, and needed to come closer to God! At the end of the sermon, he said he wanted those who desired to accept the Lord as their Savior, to come, to the adjoining tent, while **Peter and I would pray for the sick!** What a revelation! **I could call out all the different sicknesses, with Holy Spirit authority, and revelation and discernment!** Then I understood all my aches and pains, it was to be able to discern precisely, what was wrong with different people.

God healed people who had been sick for many years, and did marvelous things. "Jesus loves me, this I know, for the Bible tells me so, little ones to Him belong, **WE are weak, but HE is strong!**" Yes definitely!

When pastor Len had made the altar call, a man came for prayer, but he smelled of strong drink. After prayer, he said to pastor Len: **"Forgive me pastor, but I am now quite sober!"** He shared how **he and a friend had finished a bottle of brandy. Then they decided they were going to the tent, to see the circus.** His friend ran away while the pastor preached, but he decided to stay, therefore he got saved.

When the owners of the home came back, he was a totally changed, brand-new man. They gave their lives to the Lord, because of his testimony. They became pillars in the congregation, and serves the Lord.

Later, I longed to hear from Len and Christine, but did not know where they were with the tent. While I was praying, on a Monday morning, I saw a flying carpet. NO, NO, **I was busy with the Lord, I did not need a flying carpet.** The carpet returned again and again! Eventually, I realized that God wanted to show me something! I said: "Forgive me, if You, Lord, want to show me something, I am willing to look. I saw myself sitting on the flying carpet, and with the speed of light I traveled through the air! Soon the carpet came to a standstill, exactly where we had stayed in the caravan, next to the tent! After prayer, I phoned the pastor of that town, his wife answered. She told me that **they had just finished the tent meetings the night before.** She said, **Christine was there** with her, if I wanted to, **I could speak to her.**

We talked and rejoiced because of what the Lord had done, she then told me that many people were healed, when we were there, and were still healthy. All the glory, belongs to the Lord!

Every Monday evening, Peter and I, held a Holy Spirit Workshop, in Jan and Ria Sherman's home. It would be impossible to recount all the amazing things that happened there. I want to tell you about one.

Heather and Phil, two young converts came regularly. One night, Peter said: "One of our young ones have seen a vision. Please tell us what you have seen. No one spoke, and Peter insisted to know who saw a vision, and what the person saw, but there was still no reaction. Peter again said: "I had it so clearly, who is disobedient? Please do not be disobedient, share with us!" No one came forward.

The next week, Phil stood up, he said he wanted to confess. He saw a vision the week before, but he did not have the confidence to share it with us. During the week, however, the Lord told him to share it. He asked if he could share it with us. This is the vision.

He had low self-esteem, and had asked the Lord to reveal to him, if He had really accepted him. He wanted to know if he would be allowed to go to heaven. **He saw** a vision of **himself sitting on the**

steps of the Lord's throne, looking up at the Lord while **the Lord looked down at him with unveiled love.** This is the vision he shared.

As he was telling us about how he saw himself sitting on the steps of the throne, looking up at the Lord, **I saw the exact same vision!** Because I clearly saw the vision, **I said: "That is true!"** The moment I said that, **the big man started weeping** uncontrollably! None of us could understand what was happening.

As soon as he could speak, he told us the following. Because of his low self-esteem, he deemed himself unworthy, to sit on the Lord's throne. He wanted to share the testimony, but felt unsure. He therefore told the Lord, that he wanted confirmation, to be sure, that what he saw, was really a vision from God. **When he told us, he wanted me to say: "That is true!"** That would be his confirmation!

Amazing Grace, how sweet the sound! Indeed, how sweet it is to know that His Grace and Love never changes! The Unchanging, unfathomable riches of His Glory!

Phil and Heather, were foster parents of four brothers. They had a tremendous desire for their own children, but somehow it did not happen. The foster boys were nearly big enough to go to work, when **Heather became pregnant.** It was a joy unspeakable, and full of Glory. All of us were very excited and happy for their sake! Peter seemed to me like the fly in the ointment. I got very agitated with him! Every time I mentioned her pregnancy, he would say, that he would be the most amazed man on planet earth, if she ever had a baby!

Heather's figure got fuller and fuller, but Peter kept saying that he could not in the least understand his feelings. He only knew, that she would not have a baby!

Two weeks before her due date, she called me. She told me, that her doctor had sent her to a gynecologist, and she wanted me and Ria, to accompany her. We took her to the gynecologist, but decided to wait in the car, because his waiting room was always so full. We waited for a very long time, for her return. When at last she came, she was hysterical!

Between sobs, she told us that the gynecologist had taken a scan, and examined her, then he told her that there was **no baby! What do you say in a situation like that?** Words! Words! Words! **More than words is necessary,** but, what, and how?

Suddenly, I remembered what Peter had been saying for eight and a half months. I thought it would greatly aggravate her, but I decided to take her to my home, and I told her about Peter's prediction! Strange as it may seem, it consoled her. The knowledge that **God knew, all along,** pacified her. **This now, is the beginning of The Lord's grace and favor!** Yes, it always is : "BUT GOD!"

Phil and Heather were visiting with us, when brother and sister Verwey turned up. We had a glorious time of praise and worship. Brother Verwey came to me and asked if I had a large doll, he said he needed a large doll. I went to fetch my granddaughter's doll, and gave it to him.

He told Heather to sit down. He told her to open her arms, then he laid the doll in her arms. He said: "The Lord says, just like I laid the doll in your arms, so will the Lord lay your baby in your arms." Oh! Sweet, Sweet words for heart, hungry for a little baby to love!

They have thousands of laying hens on their poultry farm. It is approximately three miles from town. A totally strange, young woman came to Heather, on their farm, pushing a baby in a pram[a stroller]. She said somebody told her, that Heather would be willing to look after her baby for some time. She needed to go away for a few days, and was unable to take her baby with her. Heather was speechless for a while, but then she said, very unsure of the situation, that she would do it.

32

Phil and Heater stays on a poultry farm, they have thousands of laying hens. Their farm is situated about three miles from town. A totally strange, young lady came walking to the farm. She was pushing a buggy, in South Africa it is called, a pram. In the pram, or buggy was a baby boy.

She told Heather that somebody had told her, that Heather would be willing to look after her baby. She needed to go away for a while, and she would be unable to take the baby with her. Heather was bewildered, it was such a strange request, from a strange woman! She thought about it for a while, and then she consented, thinking that it would be for a short time. The woman told her to sit down, because she wanted to "**put the baby in Heather's arms**!" How about that!

The mother of the child, disappeared for a year and a half! Heather went to lay a complaint at welfare, and they eventually found out who the woman was, but not where she had gone. The baby had withdrawal signs, because the mother used drugs, while she was expecting the baby. He also was a colic baby, and cried a lot. They really had a very hard time, for the first eighteen months. Heather, was literally on day and night service!

After that long time, the mother came back, demanding the baby. The welfare told her, that she could not have the baby without a home and a proper job, because she had abandoned her baby for so long! Phil and Heather had endless trouble from the baby's mom. When Cecil was about three, his birth mother came to claim him, once more.

She proved to the welfare that she got married in the meantime, and that her husband had a steady job. **Therefore she wanted the baby!** The welfare said that they could not keep her from taking Cecil any longer, because of the proof!

A lot of Christians had promised Phil and heather that the Lord would not allow the child to be taken from them. **Now he was gone, and Phil was extremely infuriated!** He was cross about all the high hopes he had, that now came to an end. Cross about all the money they had spent, and the emotional pain, to be able to keep Cecil. Cross about the hard times they went through with the colic, and withdrawal problems. Cross that he was not there to love anymore. Cross about all the people who had told him that they would not lose the baby. Maybe, even cross with the Lord who had allowed it. He did not want to speak to anyone, or see anyone.

I heard of his pain and misery, and the Lord told me to go to speak with him. As I got to the entrance of their street, Heather came out with their car. She stopped, and I asked if Phil was at home. She told me that he was home, but it would not avail anything to go there. She said that he would not speak, to me, or for that matter, anybody else!

She just shrugged her shoulders when I told her, the Lord had sent me, and that he would definitely speak to me! There is no joy going to a situation like this. However there was so much to gain, and nothing to lose.

He met me, and because of our mutual love, I started sharing with him, that we only see as in a mirror, and do not understand. I told him that I had never prophesied to him that they would not lose Cecil. Oh I felt so awful, my heart was aching for them. I told him that **the Lord sees the end from the beginning!** That the Lord's plans and thoughts are so much different from ours. I do not remember what else, I only know that **both of us had a serious, healing bout of tears.**

One of their big foster sons was working as a male nurse at the Johannesburg Hospital. On a Saturday evening, an ambulance came to emergency, with screaming sirens! Usually, he did not go to see who came in the ambulance, **"but it so happened" that he felt very inquisitive,** and went to look! **Consternation! It was Cecil's mother!** He realized immediately, that if **she was in hospital, with an overdose of drugs, WHERE WAS CECIL?**

He called Phil, and they called the welfare. Quickly, a lot of wheels got in motion. The police went to the house from where the ambulance had taken her, to be brought to the hospital. **They found a little bundle in a corner**, staring at them through **bewildered** eyes. His nappy was caked to his very thin little body, from being whet and dry, whet and dry, and the other stuff too. There was no food, and no milk in his filthy bottle. **He was nearly starving.** He had cried so much that **he could not even cry any more.** Everything in the house was in a shambles! **God works in mysterious ways, His wonders to perform!**

That same evening, **Cecil was brought back to Phil and Heather!** This time for good! **They adopted him legally,** because his mother had no more claim to Cecil. She had no claim, because of the way she treated him!

So, you think This is the happy ending? No, not so. **It is the beginning** of something even better!

There is a chorus that says: "Standing somewhere in the shadows, you'll find Jesus—NO NOT SO! **HE is the LIGHT of the WORLD, How** on earth **could HE Possibly be in the shadows?** Shadows flee before HIM! **1John.1.5 God is light and there is NO darkness in HIM AT ALL** no not in any way! Don't look for Jesus in the dark! **Psm. 104.2 Who cover Yourself with light as with a garment—That's Jesus!**

My story, a true one, is now but halfway! Read ON, you see, this was only a few of the stumbling blocks that became Stepping Stones, in Phil and Heather's family. With Jesus, there is ALWAYS MUCH more to come!

Now for my story!" **Lord, I need to get some eggs,** I have to go to Phil and Heather!" This was Monday morning. My conversation was suddenly answered: **"Not today, not tomorrow not Wednesday on Thursday you can go"** Was the Lord's answer to my statement. I said: **"Well, if You Lord, say so,** I will go on Thursday." He said it, I believed it, and that settled it!

On Thursday, when I got to the poultry farm, I went to their home, as usual. **What I found, was not the usual at all!** Totally unusual! Their names had been on the waiting list for a baby, for very a long time. They had waited for so long, that they had just about accepted that it won't happen.

Now, Heather was sitting with a small baby in her arms. A baby bath, new bottles, small clothes, disposable diapers and everything for a new baby's arrival were all around! She looked dumbfounded! Well, I felt the same!

A placing agency had called that morning, simply telling her to fetch her baby son! She had to rush to go shopping to get all the necessary stuff. Can you? **No I don't think anybody could realize the joy she had, holding her little son**, and to know that **he is theirs**, from the start, and **for keeps!** He was just a few days old. **He became a super addition to the family!**

OH! What joy and privilege to be able to share in their happiness! This little boy **Andre', did not have the hang-ups** his older brother had! He developed beautifully, and gave them, and still gives them overmuch joy! **He definitely is his Daddy's right hand!**

Andre' could not have looked more like his Dad had Phil been his physical father! He helps with everything on the work intensive poultry farm!

Months passed, when I needed some eggs again.[I had lots in the meantime!] I have basically the same conversation with the Lord, every time I need eggs. That day He told me, I had to go on Tuesday, but I had to phone to find out if Heather was home. On Tuesday morning I phoned. She was out, but I left a message for her to call me, as soon as she got home. Later she called, and I told her that I wanted to come for eggs. She said it would be fine. I drove over to her home, and **what do you think?**

Ten and a half months later, she was holding her own lovely baby daughter! Little baby, Nicole. Basically the same happened as with Andre'. She had to go shopping again, when they called her to fetch her daughter! Nicole, has won much prizes in horse riding and jumping, her room is full of trophies, significant of her successes. You can imagine how proud the father and mother are of their children. Cecil is seventeen, Andre' is fourteen years old, and Nicole thirteen.

Their foster children are, Christian thirty five, Theo thirty four, Anton thirty three, and Frans thirty two! The foster children, are all working for themselves, and had a very good start with Phil and Heather. A lot of stumbling blocks, yes, but they became stepping stones to prayer answers!

33

Vacation! Holiday in South Africa, I heard about the differentiation in America, Government off days are called holiday! We were at a little seaside town, the translation of the name is Fleshbay! (We did not totally indulge the "flesh!)

If I wasn't writing about testimonies, I could easily be side-tracked. However let me indulge just a bit! Everything is still a little "old world" in this village. Many of the cottages still use lamps instead of electricity. The bay lends itself ideally to safe bathing in the sea. If you would climb up, or drive up the hill, the view will more than reimburse you for the trouble you had to get to the top!

OH! On some days, the sea would be azure blue, stretching to, it seemed the end of time! On stormy days, the waves would begin to chop, later huge waves would come rolling into the bay, breaking up into wild water sprays against the rocks. The cottages belonged for the most part, to farmers, some from nearby, some staying far inland. The majority came year after year, and the children and grandchildren came with them. Almost all the people, knew each other, and therefore there was a relaxed atmosphere, a joyous "don't care about tomorrow" kind of attitude. Coupled to the Christmas festivities, it was something special.

While praying one morning, I saw a vision. In the vision I saw a very tall cliff, looking as though it had been sawed off, like a slice of bread. As part of this vertical ledge, I could clearly see the layers of various kinds of stone deposits, in different colors. The layers of color in the rock, varied from brown, to reddish, to a dark brown, to yellow, to orange and other colors not so distinguishable.

I looked at this rock, and asked the Lord what He wanted to show me? There was no explanation, just another clear vision of the rock ledge. I told Peter about the vision, and I told him, that God does not have time to waste, therefore, there definitely had to be a reason, for Him to show it to me.

We had an appointment to visit a Christian family living on a farm, about thirty miles from the seaside resort. They were very sincere, lovely people. They had no pretense or showmanship. We spent a wonderful time testifying about the works the Lord, at their home, about what he did, for both our families. Before we left, we prayed together.

While Peter prayed, I saw the very same vision of the colored cliff! After prayer, I asked them if they knew about such a cliff. They said they did not actually drive around, to look at the surrounding area. (That differed totally from Peter and me.) Both Peter and I was very inquisitive, we wanted to see as much as possible, all the time.

They had a possible solution, about where the cliff might be. Somewhere on the left-hand side of the road, as we drove back, there stayed a cousin of them, but they had never been there. As far as he could recollect, there were high cliffs and mountains in that direction. He gave us the name of his cousin, if we needed to make inquiries. So we left, hoping to find the cliff the Lord had shown me! As we drove on, I told Peter to go very, very slowly, to enable me to look in the direction they told us. I had to see, if I could find the mountain and cliff.

Through the sloping from both sides, far down in a valley, for a fraction of a second, **I saw the rock ledge!** I exclaimed, there it is! When I asked Peter to reverse the car, slowly! **There was the rock ledge!** God's timing was, as usual, perfect! **The afternoon sun, lit up the rock ledge, and made it clearly visible!** Well, the Lord has definitely no interest in rocks or stones, except that the Bible says if we would not testify, the rocks or stones would call out! Maybe this one called out!

We had to look for a road in that direction. A little further, we found a road. **What a road!** It was cut out of the mountain side, and loose stones made our decent slow and dangerous. The kids shifted their weight to the side where the mountain was, as though that would steady the Kombi. Calling PA! PA! All the time, Elna was, to say the least Difficult!

At long last, we were down, off the mountain, onto level ground, we rounded a curve, and **there was the cliff!** Exactly, **precisely the way the Lord had shown me!** How exiting! More important though, was the home near the cliff! Peter asked me what we were to do. **I told him to drive to the house**, I would make inquiries, using the cousin as an excuse!

He stopped at the home, I went to the door, but before I could knock, a lady came out. We introduced ourselves, and she told me to go get my family to come on in, and have tea or coffee. She was adamant, **we HAD to come in!** She would hear of nothing contradictory! Well, that's what we wanted!

Peter and the kids came to the house, and fortunately Elna got talking to a girl. As soon as we were seated, Peter had a Word of knowledge. He asked the lady, whether she used to be a teacher? She was amazed, she said she could not believe it to be so visible after nearly twenty years had passed by!. That was, I believe the Lord's way of easing tension.

On a bed in the lounge, where we were, was a sick boy. (I thought he was the reason for our presence) He had meningitis. She told us that he had been in bed for a long time. She had not seen anybody for months, because the road did not lead anywhere else, just to their home. Her husband usually leaves at five am, to tend to his farm and animals, and he returns after sunset.

I then told her the reason for our visit, and related that the Lord had shown me a vision of the cliff, also that our friends told us to look in their direction. She started weeping. She exclaimed: **"OH! What a wonderful God we have.** This morning **I was** totally brokenhearted and depressed! **Today, precisely a year ago, my eldest son, drowned** in the Gaurits River mouth. **I felt desperate, desolate and lonely,** because it is months since I have spoken to anybody else. **Therefore I**

prayed this morning, I asked the Lord to send some of His children to me, to encourage and pray for me. Can you **imagine, how wonderful it is, the Lord sending you here, in such an amazing way, in answer to my prayer,** to come to pray for me!

We shared some testimonies with her, had tea and prayed for both her and her son. What a divine appointment! We left, feeling **over-awed by the love and compassion of our great big wonderful GOD!** He really does have a thousand miraculous ways to answer prayer! He certainly cares wonderfully for His children!

34

I promised to tell you about some humor, and here it is!

During the trip when Kobus and Norma came with us, we had to go to Vancouver. However, when we came to San Francisco, They decided to leave us to go to Europe. We had a rented car, and decided to drop them at the airport, before continuing to Vancouver.

At the airport, Kobus told Peter, before saying goodbye, they were worried. Who was going to assist me, to look after all his belongings? Norma, Kobus and I had a hard time to help the absentminded Peter, because he left everything behind. If he bought something at a shop, he would put down his camera and coat, and go off without them. He had already lost his glasses, so he could not see too well. He would have been minus many more things, had we not picked up after him!

He was quite offended when Kobus said that, and said that **he was definitely capable of looking after his own stuff!** (With my continual supervision!) Anyhow, we said goodbye to them and started our long drive to Vancouver!

We were only a few miles away, when Peter put his hand into his pocket and, OH MY! **He discovered the Motel's Key,** which I had given him to leave at reception! What to do now?

Fortunately, when I looked at the key, I saw it had a message: **"Drop in any mailbox, we will pay the postage"** That was a great help and relief!

We decided to have a good breakfast, so that we could cover as much distance as possible, while it was still daylight! We stopped at a restaurant, very near the beautiful San Francisco Bridge, and saw a red box on a pole, on the other side of the street. In South Africa, all post boxes are red, so we accepted that it was a postbox.

We had a very sumptuous breakfast, and Peter told me, that he would go over the street to put the key in the box. I told him, that I would do that, because **I did not want him to go out of my sight. He had to wait** for a moment, I just wanted to go to the restroom, I would be quick! I went to the restroom, came out, **Peter was gone!** I looked over the street, no he wasn't there! I shouted at the door of the men's restroom, No answer! Did the Rapture take place? No, certainly not, I would have gone too! I went back to the entrance, looked over to the red box, no Peter! Back to the men's restroom, maybe he did not hear me, I shouted louder PETER! **NO answer and NO Peter!**

Back to the street again, maybe he went to the car! I looked at he red box, no one! At the car! Nobody! I was feeling more than somewhat worried! **What could have happened to him!**

The night before, in our motel bedroom, we had seen **a program on TV about "fire bugs."** It was a long program, of more than an hour, offering a reward for people who would **warn the police about "fire Bugs"**

Peter, not heeding my warning, went over the extremely busy street to "POST" the motel key. He could not see very well, where the opening was, so he felt on all sides, but could not find the opening. He looked closer, and to his alarm he saw that **he was busy with,** not a postbox, but **a fire alarm!** GHEE WHIZZ! He might be reported and caught! He looked around! Yes! A man a few doors away, were watching him intently, looking at him with obvious suspicion! He went to the man, and told him that he was looking for a postbox, and since all postboxes in South Africa are red, he thought the one the pole was a postbox !

The man said: **"No ways, I have been watching you all the time! The Mailboxes in America are all blue!** There is **the mailbox** across the street, **right where you came from!"** He pointed to a large blue box. Peter, had to cross the extremely busy street, once again, the man watching him all the time! He went to the mailbox and **dropped the key inside,** thankful to be rid of it!

I looked at the other side of the street, not where our car was, OH BOY! To my relief, Peter came strolling happily towards me! I said: "Where on earth have you been?"

Suddenly I saw his knees buckle, he started pulling his hair and exclaimed: "I wish I could die right here! **Look what I have done!**" I was disconcerted, I asked him: **"What did you DO?"** He kept on moaning and groaning, then **he said: "I have just dropped the CAR key into the mailbox!"**

I laughed! and screamed With laughter! He told me to shut up! He said it was definitely not a laughing or joking matter! We had a long way to go, with a short period of time. What should we do NOW? I was tickled pink! I told him we would have to wait for the next mail collection! Peter went to the mailbox, to see what time the collection would be. He was extremely agitated, it was **only eight thirty,** and the **next collection, would only be at twelve thirty!**

Peter said to me: "We cannot possibly sit here, and wait for four hours, what if they do not come to collect?!" Then he saw a camera and film shop that was open. We went there. I was laughing all the time! In the shop he said to the man: **"Sir do you know what I have just done?"** The man answered: **"No sir, what did you do?"** Peter said: **"I just put my car keys into the mailbox!"** The man exclaimed: **"You did, You did that, hey! You put your car keys in the mailbox, HEY?"**

Peter asked him: **"Have you ever heard of anybody putting car keys into the mailbox?"** The assistant said: **"No, sir** I have never heard of anybody putting car keys into a mailbox!" Peter asked him if he would call the US Mail, to ask them to come to take the car keys out! **He said he never had reason to call the US Mail,** but he would try to do that! When he found the number in one of the directories, he called the US Mail! **He told them there's a guy who put his car keys into the mailbox, he wanted them to come to get it out!**

Obviously the person he was talking to, was very surprised, he said he too, had never heard about any one putting car keys in a mailbox!

While we were waiting for the collection man, Peter told the assistant, that **he, the assistant, must be the reason for the strange happening.** The man was taken by surprise that Peter could infer such a thing! Peter asked him if he was a Christian. He said that he belonged to the Christian Science Church. **Peter shared with him the numerical values of the Names of Jesus, proving beyond all doubt, that Jesus IS the Son of God!** Peter gave him enough to think about! He had to decide for himself, whether he was willing to accept the facts! If he accepted them, he could accept Jesus as his Lord, to become a child of God! I hope he did receive Jesus!

Within ten minutes, the US Mail pitched up! The tall, colored driver, was extremely suspicious of Peter! He said in a very heavy American accent: **"YOU the GUY that put his car keys in the mailbox?"** Peter showed him the motel key, to explain how the switch had happened. His eyes did not leave Peter's hands or body for a second. He opened the postbox, and got the keys from the bottom! He took the motel key, handed Peter the car keys, and we were literally "out" of trouble! The episode, delayed us only about half an hour, but we had something to laugh about, the whole trip to Vancouver!

It was a pleasant drive, we came to the outskirts of Vancouver, in the late afternoon. Peter wanted to go left, but I said no, we have to go right, I have prayed along the way, and asked the Lord for directions. He was unhappy with me. He said, I always wanted to do everything my own way! We are still human, and being human, we tend to "GRIND" each other. If I had not asked, and received leading from the Lord, I would have submitted to his decision!

Eventually, he said OK. Just to prove me wrong, he would go my way!! A little distance further, there was a telephone booth, in the middle of a field! What a strange place for a booth! **Maybe it was just for us to phone from!** No, probably for other people too, that also needed direction, before going to far into the city.

We phoned the people we were going to from there, they were very surprised! They wanted to know how come we got so near them. They lived less than two miles from where we were, and came to fetch us, because the last bit to their home was difficult, because the streets were not in square blocks!

While visiting there, they told us of a pastor and his wife, whom we definitely had to meet. They told us the pair had been missionaries in Africa. They thought that we ought to know them! They made an appointment for us to go to visit them. It was a real joy to meet Godfrey and Bette! They were missionaries in Rhodesia, now Zimbabwe. We invited them, and told them, should they ever come to South Africa, they were welcome to stay with us.

A few months later, to our amazement they came to see us at our home! They were asked, to care for a congregation, while the pastor was on leave, or furlough, as Americans says. When the pastor returned, they came to see us. They told us, that they felt led of the Lord, to stay in our country for a longer period of time. They asked us if they could stay with us, till it was time for them to leave. They came, and remained with us for eighteen months! God used them mightily amongst the Anglican, Catholic, Presbyterian and Charismatic churches. In eternity, it will be revealed what the impact was, they had in South Africa!

It was gratifying when later we realized the reason to go to Vancouver, was definitely Godfrey and Bette's ministry in South Africa! Thank you, Godfrey and Bette, that we could have a part in your ministry. God Bless you abundantly! Multi-purpose!

Back to Vancouver! What a wonderful time we had, we enjoyed the company, and testimonies, and they enjoyed ours! On Sunday, they told us that **they worshiped at a "High Praise" Church.** They did not know if we would find that strange. OH! Peter and I, undoubtedly, enjoyed the best church meeting we ever experienced!

Peter had our small cassette recorder, and **recorded the whole service.** During the service, there were tongues and interpretations. It encouraged us tremendously! The leading pastor's wife, had a wonderful gift from the Lord. While playing the organ, she would start to sing a new song, given to her by the Lord. Soon the congregation would be singing along! By taping the songs, we introduced many new songs to our country.

The church started early, but the anointing of the Holy Spirit was strong and invigorating, and, what seemed like fifteen minutes, were more than three hours! **We Had to leave,** because we had to drive to Seattle to be in time for our flight to Europe and home. **We barely made it!** We were truly sorry to leave, because **we had enjoyed** such **a Spiritual High in Vancouver, the place the Lord told me to go to!** How good it is when He reveals His will to us, because it works out a big blessing to all!

35

The stove in my kitchen was in front of the window, because I like to look out while cooking. While I was looking out, the scene suddenly changed! I no longer saw the trees in our garden. I was in Rome, looking down from a hill, onto the Vatican City.

I asked the Lord, what that meant. He said to me: **"Shortly you will be in Rome, then you have to go down to Palermo"** Just that! I repeated the name Palermo a few times, because I had not heard that name before! Shortly thereafter, the trip to Colorado Springs came on the agenda! We decided to do both in one trip, first to Italy, then to America.

When we got to Rome, we found that to get to Palermo, we had to either fly there, or hire a car and drive there! It was cheaper to drive there, but we had to **drive across all of Italy,** and go over to Messina with a ferry. From there we had t**o travel across Sicily to get to Palermo!** It was fun to drive through Italy, because we were able to see and enjoy the countryside. We bought the most fantastic fruit at stalls next to the road, or from farmers. Pears, apples, peaches, grapes and prunes! It was a delightful feast.

Everyday, as we got nearer to Sicily, I asked more and more urgently to know what the Lord wanted us to do there! Eventually, we knew that we would be in Palermo the next day! That evening I said to the Lord, I needed an indication, please! **The Lord said to me: "Villa Franca"** I asked if it was a small town, a business complex, or an apartment complex? No answer from the Lord!

At about three thirty, we got to the outskirts of Palermo. We went to a hotel, but they said there was a Government conference going on, and we would not find any place to stay in Palermo!

The girl at reception was very helpful and friendly. I asked if there were any Pentecostal churches in Palermo. She could not understand what I was trying to ask. At last, I drew a church spire and held my hands together as though praying. Enlightenment came to her! AH! Chiesa! SI! SI! (Hope my spelling is correct, and the word too!) She got the telephone directory, **looked up some churches,** I wrote down the names and **addresses**. We left, looking for accommodation in another hotel. OH! MY! We went from the one, to the other, and could find no place to stay. I asked an Italian for help, but he just said: **"Problema, problema! multi, multi, problema!** (Problems, problems, many, many problems)

They say Palermo was built, for the specific reason, to dodge the police. There is not a single straight street, and one way streets meet each other, head on. It is a total riddle even with a map! When we passed the same hotel, where Peter had asked for a room, for the third time, I told him to stop! He told me that it would be in vain, since he had already asked there before! I told him to give me a chance!

I went in, and asked the man at reception if he could speak English? He Waved his hand up and down, and said: **"A little bit" I showed him the couches** in the reception area, and **told him,** we have been driving around for five hours seeking a hotel, if he could not help us, **Peter and I would sleep on the couches**. He was very agitated at that! He said: "NO, NO, **I wheel fone my colleague, for place for you to stay. Vait a leetle bit!"**

He made a few phone calls, and came up with a solution. He found a room, in a hotel quite near, BUT the room had not been cleaned. IF we were willing to take that room, we were welcome! The other option was to sleep on the street in the car! I mean, that was certainly not better! They did not charge us less, even though it was not cleaned!

It was definitely one of the filthiest rooms we ever had to use. However we could have a bath and we rested warily on the used bedding!

We studied the names of the churches, and viola! The address of one church, not the kind I would ever attend, was **"Via villa Franca!"** The

name of a street! So that's it! It was our only contact of any kind! We had nothing else to follow up!

The next morning we started looking for Via Villa Franca! There is certainly NO way to describe our frustration, we drove up and down streets, **we knew where we were supposed to go,** BUT to get there was definitely something else. **After about three hours** of fruitless driving, **we saw that the street,** in which we were driving, **joined Villa Franca** at the end in a T.

Peter said to me: "I am definitely not driving into that street, it is a one-way street, and it might just be heading in the wrong direction! I will look after the car and our luggage, because everyone can see the luggage, and this is not a safe area! The Lord told you, so You **go and make your inquiries**" (We had hired a little station wagon, and all our luggage could be seen, because there was no trunk, or boot!)

It was not really MY inquiries, but I went to look for the church. I found it, but it was totally enclosed, up to the roof, with heavy, grilled iron bars. It did not look the least inviting, but **fortunately I found a bell I could ring**. I rang the bell a few times. No response! I rang again, for a longer time! **A black clad priest,** with garments reaching to the ground, **shuffled slowly to the other side of the gate!**

He greeted me in Italian, but I answered in English. I asked him, if he could understand English? He answered by holding his thumb and forefinger close to each other: **"A leetle but, If you taaak Loudly!"** I said: **"I will talk loudly!"** He told me to wait in the entrance, until he was finished with the lady he was busy talking to.

Eventually, she left, and I was seated in his office! **I asked** him, **loudly**, if there were any **Pentecostal churches in Palermo? His reaction**, in contrast to his former meek, and slow behavior, **was electric!** He nearly shouted: **"Me No Pentacostala, NO, NO, Me No Pentacostala!"** I told him that **I realized that** his church was not a Pentecostal church, **but that God had sent us to Palermo**, and **I needed to find a Pentecostal church**. He sat, shaking his head all the time, looking at me and then down to the table. He was mumbling all the time,

telling me over and over that he was not a Pentecostal at all. I kept quiet, waiting for him to calm down. **After a while I asked him, if he knew a Pentecostal church**. Very **unwillingly, he said, yes**.

I asked him **if he could direct us to the church**. Without answering, **he took out a little map**, looked at it carefully, **and indicated with red pen**, on the map, the intricate way to the other church. **If he did not do it THAT way, we would surely not have found the Pentecostal church**. So, that was the reason why the Lord had said Villa Franca. **I left, thanking him profusely, LOUDLY!**

We drove to the church, through the maze of streets, that did not make sense at all, very, very thankful for the directions! Eventually, we got to the church, it was half past one. At last after all the time, since early morning! The church was locked! I walked over the street, to where a man was working in a shop. I asked if he could understand English? He gave no sign of understanding, and waved me away! I went back, because a man was coming. I asked if he understood English? He was extremely friendly, and said he understood a bit. I showed him the church, and asked when it would be open. He showed me on his watch, half past four. He mentioned the pastor, and said: "Very nice man, Very nice man!"

We decided to look for another hotel, not in the center of Palermo. We found one, not far away, overlooking an exquisitely beautiful little bay. The rooms in the hotel were clean, quiet, and much more reasonable, AND they provided delicious food! We unloaded our luggage, cleaned up a bit, and had to leave for church again.

In my country, all prayer meetings usually are on Wednesday evenings. I was concerned about the fact that we could not make it for Wednesday. God knew that we had to be there on Thursday! Peter was worried about an interpreter. He said nobody would understand! I told him, that it was God's business, not mine, because He sent us, He would provide an interpreter!

Not long after we got to the church, the people started arriving. We asked about an interpreter. They told us there was someone who spoke

English very well! The ladies sat on one side of the isle, the men on the other. However, Peter and I sat together. As soon as the interpreter came, Peter told him that God had sent us from South Africa, we were there, but did not know what the Lord wanted to do!

When the service started, the interpreter told the congregation about us. Then they invited Peter to say something to the people. Women were expected to keep quiet. He told them, that God had actually spoken to me, and that I also had something to tell them. I told the congregation, that we were willing, after the prayer meeting, to pray for all that needed a touch from God.

When I sat down, Peter asked me if we were at the right place, I said NO! He was very disturbed! He asked me how on earth would we get to the RIGHT place, if this were not right? I told him softly, it was the Lord's business, we were obedient, we came, He, the Lord, would get us to the right place!

After the service, the total congregation came out for prayer. We were busy praying till very late. After prayer, a lady came to us, trying very hard to tell us something, but did not succeed to make us understand! Peter was tired, and wanted to leave, but she held on to me, and showed that we should wait! The interpreter, came, he said that she was inviting us to a meal at her house the next afternoon! Peter asked if she would have an interpreter, otherwise, he said to me, he would not go. I seriously wanted a nice meal! We did not understand the menus, or the names of food, we were eating hard buns every day!.

Fortunately, the interpreter said, the woman's son in law would come to interpret for us. They would come to the church to fetch us, and lead us to their home. She looked very happy when we promised to come. We slept much nicer in our new surroundings!

The next day, we drove to the church to meet the people that invited us for lunch, and drove behind them to their apartment. I had looked at all the dreary facades of the buildings. Everything seemed so old and decrepit, and therefore I felt much empathy for them. Imagine, to live in such old, old decrepit homes!

We got to their apartment building where the man had to park our car for us. They have such little parking spaces, that they are wizards to get into the tiniest place. We went through the door in the decrepit old "wall", and entered into a paradise! It was unutterably beautiful inside. The most exquisite Italian ceramic floor tiles, laid in extremely intricate patterns, the colors a blend of such rare prettiness, that I felt like Alice in Wonderland! That was only the entrance hall!

Inside the home was decorated with such subtle chick, and all the ornaments were beautiful antiques! Everything blended together to make it a lovely home, not only a showpiece. We could barely believe our eyes.

The couple, were very generous, and friendly. She had prepared a meal fit for a king! Unfortunately, we had a problem, because the son in law did not turn up! We waited for quite a while, but then she indicated that we should start eating! She still tried desperately to tell us something, while we tried to converse with hand, mouth and every possible way of making ourselves to be understood.

Peter, with his stomach full, and the "Sound Barrier" a big issue, wanted to leave. I stalled him, but just when he would wait no longer, the young man came. There had been an accident, and a traffic jam because of that!

He told us, what his mother in law, was desperately trying to tell us. The Lord had told her, she had to take us to another Pentecostal church! We agreed to meet them again in the evening, at church number one. We then went to our motel, escorted by the young man, to rest for a while.

We met at the church, and followed them to their home. We left our car there, and they drove us to the other church! Peter was again worried about an interpreter, but I told him again, that God would provide. At the church, Peter and I, met another Peter, who grew up in Chicago! He was the best interpreter I ever used!

A little while after we were seated, my Peter, wanted to know from me, if we were at the "right place." I said "YES"! Because, the Lord showed me in a vision, that everyone represented a little lamp. Over every lamp, unfortunately, hung a cloud of smoke! The flames, were obliterated by smoke. The Lord told me, if they were willing, we had to blow over the people inside the church, and the Lord would renew them. He, Himself, would blow away the smoke, and then their lights would be clearly seen by many others. God wanted to bring about a revival.

After the vision, the Italian, Peter, told us while we were waiting for the service to start, that the pastor of that assembly, was the first Pentecostal preacher that came to Sicily! He had a very, very hard time when he came. The crowds threw him with rotten vegetables, and bad eggs! They also shouted obscene things to him! His life was made nearly unbearable!

While he was telling us, the Lord spoke to me, He said: "I did not forget this pastor's labor of love, or the difficulties, and things he suffered and went through. Therefore it is only befitting, that he should be the first to hear, that I am going to do a new thing in Sicily and Palermo."

As at the other church, they gave my Peter an opportunity to talk. H e told them that God actually spoke to me, and that I would tell them what God wanted them to know.

Peter interpreted masterfully, when I delivered the above message. He told them about the smoking lamps. He said that we would blow over the congregation, if, the pastor was willing, as a manifestation, of how God wanted to blow over them. The pastor jumped up and said: "Let's Blow, Let's BLOW!"

Peter, and I, the pastor and the other Peter, blew over the hall! —Pandemonium! —All the people fell over! They were lying in their seats, on the floor and all over. God did great and mighty things, which we did not even know of! A long time later, when people got up, and "order" had been restored, we made an invitation for people to come for prayer. Just about everybody came! It was nearly twelve o'clock before we left the church! My heart was overflowing with joy! We could say like the two disciples on the road to Emmaus. Luke 24. 32 Was not our hearts greatly moved and burning within us—

We were extremely happy that we had accomplished what God wanted! The next day, started the long way back, with hearts full of thanksgiving!

Some time later, when we were in Los Angeles, we saw on the Christian channel, that God had started a new thing in Sicily! A Christian TV station started. They had no Christian material, as yet, and were asking all Christian denominations, having TV programs, to help! They had only one message. All day long, "JESUS LOVES YOU" was shown on the TV screens!

Isn't that the most important message YOU have ever heard? It certainly is for me!

Colossians 1.6 "**Indeed in the whole world (that Gospel) is bearing fruit and still is growing** (by its own inherent power), even as it has done among yourselves ever since the day you first heard and came to know and understand the Grace of God in truth. —(That is,) you came to know the grace (undeserved favor) of God in reality, deeply clearly and thoroughly, becoming accurately and intimately acquainted with it.

PURPOSE! What a fabulous word! It opens wide avenues in my mind! Who can fathom the vastness of what God wants to do! I cannot understand the **PURPOSE** of our trip to Palermo. God alone knows the **Purpose** of my life and yours, and everything!

When at last I stand before Him Who died for me, I want to be able to hear him say, that I did not live in vain. Actually, I would like Him to say, **she did what she could My best,** is maybe far worse than Your best, and my standard of achievement, far lower than yours. I only know, that He knows all things, and that gives me great peace.

36

The year 1998 was the Jubilee Year for Israel. Not for ME however. It was the steepest, of all the steep years, since the time the Lord had warned me through tongues and interpretation. It is extremely painful to relate these things.

My youngest son, Jakes, worked for a company selling car tires. The company, he worked for, treated him very well, and he was happy and encouraged. Our words, carry a weight of meaning, sometimes bringing about what we said! He told Rian, that he was so happy there, he would stay with the company, till his death!

The third week of January, although he was sick, I asked Peter to go with me to visit Jakes, Nikki, his wife, and my grandson Storm, at their home. It was a beautiful summer day. Stormy enjoyed swimming, and was showing off, to impress us! He was in and out of the pool, diving and swimming and playing on a giant tube!

Jakes, and Storm had the closest relationship I ever saw between a father and son. Not two minutes passed, or Storm would say: "Daddy, DADDY, look here!" Jakes would answer with love and patience, every time he called. We sat outside, where Jakes had pulled their fridge to clean it properly, while we conversed. He always was very helpful and caring to his wife. We had a joyful time of sharing, and we had cold drinks, and eats.

No one could have guessed, even vaguely, that it was a farewell time!

Jakes had to go to a town about two hundred miles from our home, for his company, on Thursday. On his way back home, it started to rain very heavily. People mending the road, had spilled a lot of paint on the road. When Jakes drove over the paint, his car, a new Corolla, swerved, and slid out of control! A big truck was passing, and the car

Jakes was driving, crashed into the back of the truck! The car was demolished!

The driver of the truck, said, when he stopped, and looked at the rubble of the car, that there could not possibly be anybody alive in the car! However, Jakes got out, went to the back of the car, opened the trunk(boot), in the rain, and got back in the car!

He had fetched his cellular phone. He dialed the emergency number, but before he could talk **my son Jakes died!**

The truck driver called the paramedics, and the police. While they were there, Nikki, my daughter in law, dialed Jakes, and the paramedic answered. She wanted to know what a strange person was doing with his phone. He asked, who she was, and she told him that it was her husband's phone! oh! my God! Blandly, he told her that her husband had just died, in an accident! Unimaginable! Totally, totally undesirable!

I do not intend to tell you all the details. Only know, that if you have not lost a child, you could not understand. The extremely painful anguish, the excruciating pain, and the unequaled, wrenching stab in your heart. The searing message reverberating in your mind, over and over: **Jakes IS Dead! Jakes IS Dead!**

On the twenty second January,1998, he left for heaven.

Your heart and mind tries to discard the message, but on the other hand, is the realization of the absolute inevitability, the total finality of what happened!

What is the gradient of this road? STEEP? That is an understatement! This had to be a total vertical climb, Directly into the heart of God. If not in HIS shelter, where else?

If, therefore I, who knows the Rock, experience the deadly pain of death, so most excruciatingly, what do those poor humans do, who do not have my Comforter? OH! I have a divine drive, a compulsion, a calling, and a very urgent desire, to help those in like pain, to know the only source of comfort! The everlasting arms, that hold and soothe, bringing to an aching heart **the Hope,** it is **Not forever, you will see him again!**

How do I tell my little Stormy, that his Da**ddy,** the center of his life is not here to listen to him? Will never, ever be here again? He went to sleep with his other Granny, to give his Mom time to find a measure of stability.

The next day, she and I had to go to her Mom, to tell Stormy. I had been praying for the right words to say to him ever since I heard about the accident. Nikki, his Mother, told him that there had been an accident, and that Jesus came to fetch his Daddy. Slowly, slowly his brown eyes filled with tears. He said: **"Why did Jesus come to fetch MY DADDY?"** OH! GOD! **Help! Now!** I said to him: "Would you like to have a daddy who cannot play with you?" He said : "NOOO" I said: "Would you like to have a daddy who cannot work to look after you?" He said; "NOO" I said: "Stormy, your Daddy got hurt so much, that he would not have been able to play with you, or look after you, or to work for you again. That is why Jesus took him to heaven." No, NO, not an easy road!

Were not my hand, tied to the altar, I might have slipped, or fallen! For months afterward, whenever I saw a white Corolla, I would burst out in tears. Once when the pain was so overwhelming, I asked the Lord, why did He not comfort me? He said to me: "My child, TIME is My best comforter!" Yes, that certainly, is true. However, the longing, the loss, is with me always! I tell the Lord ever so often, to give Jakes my regards and my love!

Peter, never got over this pain. He became more and more sick, and withdrew himself from everything. So I was alone and lonely, although I had a husband.

Some time after Jakes went to be with the Lord, my friend Faith Honey, (a good combination for a name and surname!) had a dream. She became aware of something smelling very nice. Jakes was standing in front of her bed, with a big bunch of sweet smelling red roses. She asked him what he was doing there, and why did he have the roses? He told her, that he brought the roses for her. He said he brought it for her, because she always talked to me and consoled me. He told her, that she had to tell his Dad, that his Mom was terribly, terribly lonely! His Dad had to get out of bed, help me with the business and live with me." Unfortunately, Peter was in too much depression to heed this warning.

A while later, she had a second very vivid dream! She was walking in heaven with Jakes, suddenly they went through a passage, and on the other side, was a patch of exquisitely beautiful roses. She went to the rose tree, to smell some of the roses. Jakes thanked her again, for being my friend and they talked about the beauty of the roses. He was carrying a Bible.

Suddenly he said: "I have to leave, I have to go." She asked him: "Where do you have to go to?" He said: "I have to go to a meeting." She was surprised and asked him: "What kind of a meeting, do you have to go to?" He answered: "Aunty Faith, **I did not read the Bible while I was on earth, I now have to study The Bible!** I must go now!' He left her, and she woke up.—

I am studying the Bible here, before I might discover, in heaven just how much I lost, because I did not know the precious promises in the Word of God!

The crime rate in South Africa is very high! The walls around the homes and apartments gets higher and higher. Motorcar theft, and hijackings is not something scarce and rare anymore! Therefore, my son Karel applied for, and got work in the USA. He should have left in February 1998. Because of what happened to Jakes, he asked for a postponement. His new job, overseas, told him that they would postpone it till August 17 1998. Should he not keep to that date, he would be liable for a large fine!

Karel used to work in Sandton, an expensive, top class, area. On June first, 1998, he was hijacked in Sandton. Black men, drove past, swerved in front of him, and told him to get OUT! The three of them, took his car, an expensive BMW, his cell and all his other stuff, and drove off, leaving him dazed and frightened!

When he got to a place where he could phone the police, they asked him if he was OK. He said Yes! They told him, that he was very lucky, he was the the fifty seventh person to be hijacked in Sandton, that day. Seven were shot dead!

He did not want to tell me that evening, but when he phoned me the following day, it was a terrible shock! I nearly lost another son! The could-have been, had me in agony, until the sweet Holy Spirit spoke to me, and told me to be realistic. **It did not happen!** Karel, had nightmares for weeks! He would wake up totally drenched in sweat, after a bad nightmare!

That was not to be the end of the enemy's jubilee year. The Lord had quickened to me, that Cherie, Karel's wife was pregnant. He told me every time I mentioned it, that there was nothing of the kind. He ascribed her behavior to stress, because of the going to America, and stress to leave her family!

On Thursday, the thirty first August, I visited Cherie at their town home. She said to me: "MAM, my nerves must really be in a bad condition! I keep nibbling on anything I see. It's so totally unlike me." I kept quiet. But after I left her, I called Karel with my cellular phone. I congratulated him, once more, and told him he was going to become a Daddy! Again he assured me that it was NOT the case. I asked him to get a test apparatus on his way home, to settle our argument!

The following morning, **the result of the test, was positive**. That caused a new outlook on their departure. It was exceedingly difficult for Cherie, to leave everything that was familiar, and all her family. So hard, to go to a strange country, with no security. Nobody to turn to, for advice or help, and all alone during the day, in the strange place. By the Grace of God, and with His help, she came through, tops!

Peter, was in a bad way. A month or two before, he had a terrible headache during the night. We did everything possible, but it would not budge! Eventually, he said it felt as though he was having a stroke.

SO often, we are too close to our problems, our perspectives then, are not clear and true.

After that headache, he complained that he could not think in his head clearly. Therefore he wrote ceaselessly, and would tear up what he wrote. Because he had been ill, stressed, and depressed for so long, I did not heed it as much as I should. The impending move of my kids to America, and the business I had to do by myself, kept me busy.

On Friday, he was totally stressed, and told me that he did not want to live any longer! I tried to reason with him, but it did not avail anything. I had to take care of things that could not wait. Friday, and Saturday and Sunday were three nightmare days. Quite a few people came to pray, and reason with him. He told everybody that he was already dead, they just did not understand, he appreciated their concern, but he had already died! Nothing, could be done for him, he was already dead! He did not want to go to the doctor. He said nobody could do any thing for him.

Monday morning, I was desperate. I phoned my friend Faith, and told her to be ready at eight, I wanted to fetch her, that we could agree, and pray for Peter. He was very glad and anxious to get me to go, to fetch her! He said it was a good thing that I wanted to fetch her!

When I got to her home, she was not ready! I had a red-hot, burning haste in me, but she was in no hurry. Eventually, I told her that I was leaving without her. She jumped in and at breakneck speed I raced home!

At our apartment, I ran into the building. Oh! dear god! **How awful! My sweetheart,** for whom I had fought so hard, **was DEAD! This time not only spiritually, but also physically! Gone beyond reach!**

The **whole world exploded!** What a terrible, terrible, searing explosion! My world, my whole existence, was totally shattered!

A man asked me how I felt at that time! Not he, not you, not anybody dare to want to know! There is **absolutely nothing**, absolutely **no way**, to describe what I felt. I do not even want to try! God alone knows how very, very steep it was! I thought: **Oh! God! Will I ever be able to come to the end of this road?** It seems to be never ending!

God gave me mercy, therefore I had hoped and believed, believed again, and again that the next day there would be change for the better. (A prophetess called me, during a church meeting, and told me that God had told her to pray for me, for the **wounds of disappointment!** There were SO many, scores and scores of them!)

Never, ever can I forget the way everything caved in under me, when I came back, and he had passed away! It was as though the earth opened, and I were falling down a bottomless pit! I cried out to God! I said to Him **I do not know how to take the next step.** I am **not able** to make the next step! I do NOT know HOW to carry on! I do not want to carry on! **I am too Shattered!"** I was devastated because in my mind I knew that I had come to the total, final,end! **I was totally incapable to carry on**! I was the broken vessel of the potter! He alone could make me over anew!

My merciful heavenly Father had given me a wonderful heritage from my Mother. Like in **Psm 51.12 "Restore to me the joy of your salvation, and grant me a willing spirit to sustain me."** This willing spirit, was now not sustaining me, anymore! It had failed, completely, because it was my spirit **not His Spirit!**

oh! Precious, Precious Father! what joy! a joy surpassing ANY JOY, I ever had, **ever** had **experienced**, flooded my soul! It was **so overwhelming** that I could not contain it! **God in His unfathomable mercy** spoke to me! He said to me:

"**My child, you** thought that it was for punishment, that I wanted to take Peter home the 1s^t April 1972, my child, **it was not for punishment**! I, **Who knows all things beforehand, love you so much,** that **I wanted to spare you all** disappointments, heartaches, losses, misery, loneliness and every negative thing, that happened to you, because he did not leave that time! **Had he gone home** that time, **none of these would have happened. You would have been spared all,** because **I love You so much.**

w unfathomable, the riches of his love, and care! In an instant, His willing Spirit, gave me strength and joy! God loves me so much Oh Thank You Lord **Merciful, Merciful God!** In MY ignorance, **I knew better.** Wanted it MY way! I was like the Israelites, yea sure, their desire was granted, but they also got a leanness in their soul.

For twenty six, long years, I reckoned myself responsible for Peter, had I not prayed him back? All the time I tried to stand in the gap for him. All those years, he was never healthy. All that time he was depressed, and suffered, and wanted to go to the Lord. It was MY fault! He was MY responsibility. I tended to his every wish. Tried every doctor. Tried every medication. Nursed him from seven in the morning till nine o'clock at night, during his operation for a diaphragm hernia. Nursed him at home all his life!My God, **how I hoped** that he would be well!. But, no Nothing changed or helped! Hope would flare up, for disappointment, to take over again.

Our dear God, had been waiting for me, to come to the end of myself. **My** schemes, **My** endurance, **My** ability to keep on keeping on! **Waited** for **Me** to come to know that I could **not** carry Peter! I was not his salvation! The enemy used my guilty conscience to punish me!

Ps. 49.7 **"No man [or woman]can redeem the life of another** or give to God a ransom for him 8. The ransom for a life is costly, no payment is ever enough" (**Jesus alone is able** to ransom a life, by His own blood.)

I had a lot to work through. After all my labor of love, all my support, all my sacrifices, for so many years, it still were in vain. Not instantly, no, slowly, slowly, I came through! Even anger towards myself, I had to forgive myself too. All, in our total **life, is a matter of Choices!**

I had to choose to forgive Peter. I had to forgive him, even though he was not with me. I had to forgive him and myself, from my heart. Matt. 18.32 then the master called the servant in. "You wicked servant," he said "**I canceled all that debt of yours because you begged me to.**

33.Shouldn't you have had mercy on your fellow servant just as I had on you? 34. In anger his master **turned him over to the jailers to be tormented, until he should pay back all he owed. 35. this is how my Heavenly Father will treat each of you, unless you forgive** your brother **from your heart!**

The torturers, oh no! I had to decide, and I could choose to stay bitter and unforgiving, and be handed over to the torturers. Bitterness and an unforgiving lifestyle, is the main cause of arthritis. NO! I did not want that torture, I had to accept the only way of escape! Forgive! From my heart! I did that, totally! I just have a very big regret, that he never used his God-given abilities rightly.

Disappointment! OH! I have to say truthfully, that in unguarded moments, this torturer, still sometimes surface! I can say, before God, that **I had tried so hard!**

I was striving endlessly, on my own, with countless efforts. I wanted to be fruitful for the Lord! I desired to do more for Him! I longed to BE and To DO! But was always in bondage to an unwilling partner. I could do only as much as he would allow. I continually tried to enlarge the terrain! I was like a doggy on a leash! I wanted to break free, to RUN! Yes, I am still disappointed, but now I am healed, and are going to rush as fast as the Lord would permit me to go, I am on His leach now!

Need! I had no income, and because of wrong decisions he had made, we had lost all the money we had inherited. I prayed, and in answer to my prayer God gave me the dream and business, that the book starts with. Once again, I worked very hard. I wanted to prove that **I could make it.** I worked twelve to eighteen hours per day! I toiled endlessly, day in, day out. Not only for the secular work, but as much as I could, for the Kingdom too!

When Peter was living and always ill, always in bed, I was very lonely. I said to my friends, that I was very lonely **with** him. It would be better, if I were able to go to one of my many, many friends, if I did not have to look after him! Ignorance! Oh yes, but No bliss! I found, to my amazement, that all the many friends, were busy with their own problems, and households. So, I realize why God laid the lonely people on my heart.

,I am going to work for the Lord with more untiring devotion than for the business. **He is able to make all grace abound to you, so that in all things at all times, having all that you need, you will abound in every good work**! 2.Cor. 9. 8 AMEN! SO BE IT!

Please take note, this is NOT a pity party! I was willing to share this experiences with You! I do not know, God alone knows, **who** has to benefit from MY learning processes! It is not easy to bare your soul, even before your best friends! To do that to the "world" was, the steepest part of the book.

May God, the Author and finisher of all things, **use the stumblingblocks, He carried me over**, and that **He changed into Stepping-Stones**, help **you** to realize, that **there is nothing too hard for Him!** Time is so short before the coming of Christ, take hold of His hand, **He is able** to carry you through.

Instead of saying: **"Why pick on ME!"** Know, that He Who sees the end from the beginning, has a reason for allowing stumbling blocks in your life. You cannot have understanding of another's pain, if you have not walked in his, or her shoes. However, I think the prayer, "God grant me the courage to change the things I can, and to accept the things I cannot change, and the serenity to know the difference." is maybe a good starting point.

I can truthfully say: **"I do not know what the future holds but I know who holds the future!** It gives me joy unspeakable, and I am full of expectations! God healed a lot of people by His gifts, operating through me, and the word says that His gifts is without repentance. Therefore, I liked to be away from my everyday stressful situations, but **I am looking forward to the enfolding of His plans for me, with great expectation!**

Hallelujah! Praise the Lord! I can see, I can walk, I enjoy food, **I enjoy His Favor,I enjoy** humor, **I enjoy** laughing, most of the time for my own blunders! I still feel as a teenager inside, **expectation is alive** in me! **Hope is alive** and well in me! **Love is alive** and well in me! Yes **God is alive in me!** My heart overflows with gratitude! He knew what kind of surgery to use, to cut out all the unnecessary dross of my life! **In Him I live, and move and have my being!**

My text from the Bible to live by is this: "**Blessed – happy, to be envied – is she who believed that there would be a fulfillment of the things that were spoken to her from the Lord.**" Luke 1.45 Therefore I choose to believe, all the time! AMEN

The last two Chapters of the book, I promise you, will be a big blessing to You! Read about the two **amazing testimonies, of Frank and Frankie.**

37

People of all ages, all walks of life, and all nationalities, came to our Holy Spirit Workshops! Some came once, for a specific need, and never again. Others came regularly, drawn by the sweetness of God's Presence, or by the wonderful, miraculous ways God worked. One couple who came regularly was Frank and Chrisma!

Frank, was a very quiet person. He did not have the gift of the "GAB." If you did not speak to him, he would sit for hours without saying anything. Chrisma, on the other hand, made up for his reticence! She loved to testify, and bubbled with zeal, for the Lord!

They both grew up in a traditional church. They came to know the Lord in the latter part of their lives. They had a brown dog, he had arthritis in an advanced stage. I often wondered why they did not put him to sleep. Then Frank retired from work and he started delivering spiritual pamphlets! We call it "tracts" in South Africa! The dog faithfully accompanied him on his rounds. Anyone suffering from arthritis, please note, the exercise had him fit in three months time!

Chrisma, asked us to pray for Frank, because he had terrible pain in his stomach. I told him, we would pray for him every week till he had victory! This we did for about four weeks. On a Saturday evening Chrisma phoned us. Frank had been admitted to a hospital, and he desired, that we should come to pray for him! It was already a bit late, but we decided to go.

At his bedside, **I Knew** without a shadow of a doubt, **that he was going home** to be with the Lord. I had the greatest possible desire to send love and greeting to those who had already departed earlier! However, I thought it would be inappropriate to do that. We anointed him with oil, [I knew it was in preparation for his departure,] and prayed for him!

In the car, Peter confirmed that he too knew that Frank was going "HOME!" During the early hours of Monday morning, he went to be with the Lord! Chrisma, informed us that the funeral would be on Wednesday morning.

On the way to the funeral, we talked about the strange circumstances. It would be a traditional congregation in a Pentecostal church, and we wondered how that would be. It would be especially strange for the family from traditional churches,on both sides!

Shortly after we were seated in church, the Lord told me that He wanted me to speak in tongues. It happens very rarely at a funeral, that a message in tongues is delivered. I did not care, even if it was rare, what the Lord wanted, was all that mattered. I asked the Lord to reveal to me, when I had to speak. The congregation started to sing a hymn, and I saw a vision.

I saw Frank and his dog, at the beginning of a very long street. I experienced a tiredness, of such total intensity, that it was like an acute physical dehydration. I knew that was the way Frank felt! I saw him looking at the LONG street before him, and heard him say: "I have to go up this street, and come down the other side." **He had a goal, and he forced himself to accomplish that**. There was a lull in the proceedings, and the Lord said to me: **"Now!"**

I stood up, and spoke in tongues, the Lord gave me a very clear utterance. Peter, had a fright when I suddenly broke the silence. The pastor, a wise man of God, spoke to the congregation. He told them, that what they had just heard, was the strange tongues the Bible talks about. He said, for the unenlightened he wanted them to know, **if they opened their Bibles to 1 Cor. 14.** They would be able to read more about that. He also said that he realizes in his spirit, that God had an interpretation for the tongues, and asked the person with the interpretation to be free and obedient to bring it.

Peter, after his initial shock, because it is so very unusual received the interpretation and told us the Lord said the following: "It is by the greatest exception, that the Holy Spirit give a testimony at the funeral of a deceased. And the testimony of the Holy Spirit is two fold. **Firstly! Frank M Loved ME, to his utmost,** dearly and sincerely, and **with his whole heart! Secondly!** Frank M, **You Were Faithful with a Few, things I will put you in charge of many things Just that!** [Matt.25.21]

It was wonderful, but seemed a bit irrelevant. After the service we went to the graveyard to finish the burial. When that was over, on our way to our car, Chrisma, called and came running towards us.

When she got to us, she exclaimed: "OH! Brother Peter, thank you so much for the interpretation! It was the most wonderful interpretation I have ever heard! Frank got truckloads of pamphlets (tracts) that he delivered. He went through our city three times. Sometimes he came home, heartbroken, when a person flung the tract down, or told him to keep his own rubbish! He exerted himself tremendously, most of the time he was totally overexerted, and would be so extremely exhausted, that he could barely walk into the house.

When I chided him not to exert himself like that, He would say to me, every day without exception: "Chrisma, you know, I cannot talk. You know I cannot testify. This is the only thing that I can do for the Lord. I love the Lord sooo much, and when I get to heaven, **all I want the Lord to say to me is: Frank M over few you were faithful, I will appoint you over much!**

Just that! Well, all I can say is that God's scales weigh totally different from our human ones. He seemed such an insignificant man to many. How glad I am, that **Our Heavenly Father** sees our hearts. **He does not judge a book by its cover,** as we so often do. His perception and thoughts about people are totally different from ours.

So many people find tongues and the interpretation of **tongues a stumbling block** All I can say is, God used the stumbling block, to confirm to Chrisma and all others who have heard the testimony, that He hears and answers prayer. He answered Frank's prayer!

I not need God to prove to me to me, that **His Word is the highest authority in the whole universe!** I have accepted that, if maybe you have not realized it yet, please, please, do not allow, tradition, unbelief, doubt, fear, peoples opinions or anything else to rob you of your inheritance! I cannot strongly enough press it onto your heart!

Peter and I did not know about Franks delivery efforts or exhaustion, or about his outspoken verbal desire or that he wanted God to say to him: **"Frank M over few you were faithful, over much will I appoint you!"** Can you possibly try to understand, OH! My heart, and my whole being, can barely contain the awe, Love, reverent fear, gratitude, appreciation, amazement and exuberant joy, about the reality, that Frank M, heard the MASTER acknowledge him, like he had asked, openly before all. He was such a nondescript man, ignored and despised by many. **AND YET! there is nothing Hidden from His all-seeing eyes, not even an "Unimportant" man!**

He, Our God, knows the intents and purposes of your hearts. **HE knows even your thoughts from afar of!**

Dumbfounded, I want to prostrate myself before This Awesome GOD! I want to lose myself in the depths of His Unfathomable Love! A GOD, Oh! what a God! A GOD, Who sees, and knows, the end from the beginning, for Whom nothing is too small or too difficult. I want to stop trying to REASON with my puny little understanding, "Why This Why That, **"Why is this in the BIBLE?"** Father GOD, **I Accept Your Word exactly as it is written, with all my heart, it is My inheritance I will not** allow anyone, or anything, to rob me of a single one of the promises in Your Word!

I do not endeavor, to bring you dear reader, clever thoughts or teachings, I only state emphatically, with truth, facts that corresponds with reality, this is definitely what happened.

When we stand before HIM, he will ask: "Did you Read My Will And Testament? **Did you believe what was written therein?** Did you understand the provisions. Did you accept all I told you? Did You comply to the provisions? Then you may inherit!

In South Africa, the Government Gazette has scores of unclaimed inheritances, of people who do not know about the inheritance, therefore they do not inherit! Read your NEW Testament! Every will has provisions, how strange they may be, and if not conformed to, nobody may have, or enjoy the inheritance.

Please become obedient, and accept your inheritance! All has been paid for.

38

This testimony, I heard from Keith, the Executive Director of a wellness company, here in America.

The company had opened a branch of the business in Mexico, and Keith had to go to help with administration. Because it is so excessively warm in daytime, the Mexicans takes a siesta, or rest during the day, and work much later at night. Keith, however started very early and worked right through. After a week of the strenuous schedule, he was extremely tired.

When he had to return, he decided to take the last flight, but to go the airport early. He wanted to board as soon as possible, to be able to relax in his seat. At the airport, after receiving his boarding pass, he asked the flight attendant, to try to keep the seat next to him open. She told him that it was a fully booked flight, therefore she could not promise, but she would try, to keep the seat open! He sat down, and allowed his tired body to start relaxing.

Just when he was dozing off, the attendant, tapped him on his shoulder, and told him that she needed the seat next to him. A young boy of about eight, moved into the seat next to him. Keith realized that it could mean interruptions of his desired rest, therefore he closed his eyes immediately.

Allow me, at this time, to bring a tribute to Keith. I came to know him in South Africa, because we also have this remarkable business over there. Keith, is one of the nicest and most courteous Christians I have ever met!

A few minutes later, the boy tapped him on his arm, and asked him, what his name was. He told the boy that his name is Keith, and asked the boys' name. He said his name is Franky, and asked if Keith was also going to Dallas? Keith told him, that he too was going to Dallas. But he had a very hectic week, and he was very, very tired and would like to rest a bit, if Franky would please excuse him. So, Keith, tried once again to rest. Soon after the plane was airborne, he heard the trolley with the drinks coming.

The stewardess said: "Excuse me sir, would you like something to drink?" Keith kept quiet, but not our little friend! He said: "I don't think Keith would like something to drink, he is very, very tired, he has had a hectic week, and would like to rest a bit, **but I would like a coke please.**" Keith heard Franky's table being lowered, and Frankie then received and thanked the stewardess. The cart passed **but** within a minute! **Franky's coke was all over Keith!** He jumped up, the stewardess tried to dry his clothes, while all the time **Franky was profusely asking Keith to forgive him, for putting the coke all over him.**

Keith assured Franky, that, he was not cross with him, because an accident can happen to anybody! When the drying process was over, Keith sat down to resume his pursuit of rest again!

Who can keep a cork under water? **Who can keep an excited youngster quiet?** A few minutes later, he tapped Keith on his arm once more, he said: **"Keith, you must be mad at me** for putting the coke all over **you!"** Once more Keith reassured him that he definitely weren't cross with him. By then, **Keith came to realize, that there must be a divine purpose for them to be together,** especially after Franky's next questions.

"Keith, is somebody coming to fetch you on the airport?" Keith answered: "No Franky, I left my car at the airport, I am driving home with it. **Is somebody coming to fetch you at the airport, Franky?"** "Yes, Keith my Mom is coming to fetch me at the airport." Keith said: **"Your Mom must be very happy to get you!"** Forlornly, Franky answered: "As a matter of fact, **Keith, I don't think so.** My Mom needed time to adjust to her new husband, that is why I stayed with my Dad in Mexico for two years." "OH" Keith answered: "Then your **Dad must be very sorry to have you go back** to your Mom!" **"NO,**

Keith, I don't think so. **My dad is getting married,** and the lady he is marrying, has children of her own, so **there is no more space for me."**

We sing, about broken pieces, **No! It is broken people!** Keith realized then, that God made the appointment for the two of them, to sit next to each other. The angels, must have put the coke All over him!

Keith, started to share with this piece of broken humanity. He told Franky, that **God does not make "nobodies," HE only makes "somebodies,"** and that he, **Franky was not a nobody, he was a somebody. and** that **he, Franky,** could change the whole world, **well, if maybe not the whole world,** he could **at least change the world he lives in.**

Because this was during a business motivational address, Keith did not tell more about what he shared with Franky.

However, all to soon he heard the captain, telling them to fasten their seat belts for landing in Dallas, Fort Worth. Quicker than any flight before had ever seemed to pass!

A flight attendant, came round and told Franky to remain seated when the plane came to a standstill, and to wait till all the passengers had left. She would then come to collect him. Quickly he reiterated: **"Oh! no! That won't be necessary, my friend, Keith,** here, **will take me!"** Already, a heavenly bond, of love and trust, had been established between Keith and Franky!

They got off the plane, collected their luggage, saw how all the passengers, also the flight attendants, and finally the captain and crew leave. They were the only persons remaining, since it was the last flight, and **there was No sign of his Mom!**

Keith said: "Franky, it seems to me that **we have a bit of a problem!** Do you have your Mom's telephone number? He answered: "Unfortunately, not Keith!" "Do you have your Dad's number?" Franky answered: "Yes I do, Keith, but it won't help us any, because my Dad got married today, and they left on their honeymoon. There isn't anybody at home!" "Well" Keith said: "let's look through your luggage, maybe your dad did write your Mom's telephone number somewhere, so that we can contact her!" Fortunately, they found the Mom's number, and called her.

She was extremely agitated and said that her ex had not told her, that he would put "**the child**" on the plane that day, she was only expecting "**the child**" the next day! Keith then told her, that he could bring Franky home,because he had his car at the airport, but she told him to stay right there, **She would come to fetch him**. However, it would take her, an hour and a half, to two hours to get to the airport. Thus, Keith had a longer time, to share with Franky about the Lord. Eventually the Mom came, not even thanking Keith very nicely,and with a huff and a puff she was gone with Franky. **End of the story? No, not by any means!.**

A few weeks later, in the midst of a very important meeting, Keith's secretary interrupted the meeting. She said: "I am very sorry, to interrupt, Keith, but **there is a guy** on the line, **he won't take No! for an answer. He said he is your friend, and that you definitely will speak to him!**" "Oh" Keith asked: "**And who is this friend,** that I definitely will speak to? "Well" she said, "**He says, his name is Franky!**" "Yes!" exclaimed Keith: "**He IS my friend, and I definitely Will speak to him!**"

Franky, came on the line and said: "Keith, **I want you to know, that I have adjusted extremely well to my step-father, and I *have adjusted extremely well to my Mom*,** and I have adjusted extremely well in my new school. **I have never, ever been so happy in all my life.** My Mom is here, she also wants to talk to you."

The Mom came on the line and said: "**Keith, I do not know what you told my son. He walks around** all day, **telling everybody, that God does not make nobody's, He only makes somebody's,** and that he, Franky, is NOT a nobody. He also says, that **he can change the whole world. And,If maybe he cannot change the whole world, at least he can change the world he is living in!**

I want to thank you from the bottom of my heart, because **I cannot tell you, what a big change, Frankie has made in our lives!**

Beloved, what is happening in your world? Are you changing it for the better? **For whatever you sow, that you will surely reap!** Always remember, if you **sow one grain you will reap at least a hundred good or bad seeds!**

In parting, **if you** don't have a **smile,** I definitely, **would love to let you have one or more of mine!** Because **He turns all** of my **stumbling blocks into stepping stones,** I am Not at all short of smiles, and between the **S** and **S, is a mile** of smiles Bless You Abundantly, **I hope to meet You, either here or in Heaven. I believe you realized : "Heaven! That's where I am heading!"**

In every victory, let it be said of Me, in Christ alone, do I put my trust! Bye!

0-595-25013-0